The Young

Bilbury Days

Vernon Coleman

Another collection of memories from the English village of Bilbury.

Note: As usual, the names and details of individuals, animals and establishments, except the Duck and Puddle and Peter Marshall's shop, have been altered to protect the innocent, the guilty and those who aren't quite sure where they stand but would like to think about it for a while. The events in *Bilbury Days* occurred in the 1970s.

The Author

Vernon Coleman qualified as a doctor and practised as a GP. He is a *Sunday Times* bestselling author who has written over 100 books which have been translated into 25 languages and sold in over 50 countries. His books have sold over two million copies in the UK alone though no one is sure whether two million people each bought one book or one person has a very large bookcase. Vernon Coleman is also a qualified doctor. He and his wife (whose real name is Antoinette) live in Bilbury, Devon, England. Vernon is an accomplished bar billiards player (three times runner up in the Duck and Puddle Christmas competition), a keen but surprisingly dangerous skittles player and an accomplished maker of paper aeroplanes. He has a certificate proving that he once swam a mile for charity. He was, at some point in the early 1960s, second in the Walsall Boys Golf Championship and was awarded with three brand new golf balls in a smart, cardboard box. He claims to be one of the best stone skimmers in North Devon. (Nine bounces are by no means unheard of and he has a personal best of 12 bounces.) He is a long-term member of the Desperate Dan Pie-Eater's Club (vegetarian section) and although he can juggle three balls at once, he cannot knit. He has never jumped out of an aeroplane (with or without a parachute) but he has, on several occasions, lit bonfires in the rain and is particularly proud of the fact that he once managed to light one in a snowstorm. He has not yet availed himself of the extensive opportunities apparently offered by social media (he says he is waiting to see if the idea catches on) but notes about important events are pinned on the noticeboard outside Peter Marshall's shop in the village and he has had a website (www.vernoncoleman.com) since the day after King Alfred burnt the cakes. Entrance to the website is free of charge and there is ample parking space. Visitors to the site are requested to wash their hands before entering and to wipe their feet before leaving. Sadly, there are no advertisements or refreshment facilities. The Author is registered as an Ancient Monument and selected parts of him are Grade II listed.

ernon Coleman's novels include: *Mrs Caldicot's Cabbage War*, *Caldicot's Knickerbocker Glory*, *Mrs Caldicot's Easter Parade*, *Mr Henry Mulligan*, *The Truth Kills*, *Second Chance*, *Paris in my Springtime*, *It's Never Too Late*, *The Hotel Doctor*, *My Secret Years with Elvis* and many others. All of these books are available as e-books on Amazon as are the books in The Young Country Doctor series.

The Young Country Doctor series

This is the 14th book in the series and so, if the author has done his sums right, there are probably around thirteen other books describing the Devon village of Bilbury and its inhabitants. All the books in the series are available as e-books on Amazon. A few hardback editions of the first seven books were self-published in modest runs but these are all now out of print. The first few books are sequential but after about the third book you can read them in any order you like without getting into a tangle. Film companies should know that Thumper Robinson and Patchy Fogg are both happy to play themselves if a movie is made. Frank and Gilly are prepared to make the Duck and Puddle available to filmmakers, and I can confirm that they make excellent sandwiches and serve wonderful beer. Peter Marshall, who runs the Bilbury village shop, would like to talk terms before making a decision about his participation but no one in Bilbury doubts that he would jump at a chance to promote his shop on the big screen. Publishers and film companies wanting to get in touch with the author should pop a note into a bottle, throw it into a nearby waterway and wait for a response.

Dedication

To Antoinette: You will forever fill my heart and nothing will ever change that truth. Everything else is just noise.

Foreword

I made a catapult the other day. I don't know why. I didn't need a catapult. I didn't even want one. Not really.

What happened was that after cutting some dead birch branches and some coppiced hazel sticks into kindling, I found myself left with a forked piece of wood that was simply crying out to become a catapult. It was far too nicely shaped to end up on the fire. So, I found a thick piece of elastic that had once been something else and five minutes later I had a simple but effective catapult.

I obviously then had to make a bow and arrow.

And for that I needed a suitably sized branch of ash, a few nice straight pieces of bamboo and some bird feathers (willingly donated by various visitors to our garden). The only other requirement was a reasonably sharp penknife.

Looking back, it is astonishing how much of our time at school was spent in pastimes which would be considered unacceptably violent today. Every boy I knew carried one or two strong rubber bands in his blazer pocket. These were used to fire paper pellets at terrifying speed. When soaked with ink from the inkwell in the top right hand corner of every desk these pellets left their mark in more ways than one.

As I looked at my newly made catapult, I found myself drifting back to another world, another life, another era and it occurred to me that although many older readers of my Bilbury books will recognise and understand the world I am describing, younger readers may find it difficult to believe that there was a time, not so long ago, when the world was very different and was, in many ways, a more dangerous place.

At the grammar school which I attended, school teachers were frequently violent; smacking pupils around the head so hard that the victim would be dazed and semi-conscious for most of the rest of the lesson. Even at the age of 14, I spotted that there didn't seem to be much point in shouting at a boy for not paying attention and then hitting his head so hard that he didn't know where he was. Some teachers used their hands as weapons while others preferred to use special, long, steel edged rulers. All those practitioners of the backhand and forehand head-slap were probably excellent tennis players. One, I remember, specialised in a backhand, forehand, backhand triple slap. The unfortunate recipient would be dizzy for the rest of the day.

Other teachers liked to throw things. Heavy, wooden board rubbers were especially popular weapons and would be hurled at maximum velocity. The teacher's desk contained a box of sticking plasters for those boys who were too slow or too distracted to duck. This sort of steady bombardment was considered normal, and an essential part of the school day. In every classroom where I studied, the plaster of the back wall was pock marked as though it had been subjected to machine gun fire.

Toy manufacturers made most of their products out of lead and then coated them with lead paint so that when children sucked the toys, they could get their daily dose of lead without doing too much damage to the toy itself. I always preferred the blue lead myself but this was just a personal preference. A chum of mine used to like biting the heads of lead soldiers but I think this was a private idiosyncrasy and I have no knowledge of it being widespread. Just about every toy made in the 1950s was sexist, racist or dangerous. Boys had guns and soldiers, and girls had dolls and prams and everyone thought that was right and proper and what else could you possibly expect. Sharp edges were so common that I now suspect that toy makers were instructed to build in the sharp edges so as to ensure a steady supply of business for sticking plaster manufacturers. When, as a small boy, I went surfing at Treyarnon Bay in Cornwall, my parents rented for me a surfboard made out of a plank that had not been properly planed. The edges were rough and splintery and at the end of a day in the sea, I would go back to our caravan bleeding from a thousand cuts. Fortunately, the Cornish sea was clean enough in those days to sterilise the wounds. I'm not sure I would trust myself to its cleansing nature these days. Today, anyone renting out such equipment would be dragged through the streets by appalled health and safety officials. But I bet I had as much fun on my plank as any surfer has today on one of these specially made and contoured boards.

8

When I was a boy, in the 1950s, I spent my summer holidays exploring, making camp sites, lighting fires, tearing my trousers on barbed wire and falling off my bicycle. My mother must have spent a good chunk of housekeeping on plasters, bandages and iodine.

But at least I was out of doors and most of the games we played were free and some of them really did grow on trees. Old bits of string and shoelace were kept for stringing conkers from September through to December.

Pocket money was spent on comics, marbles, small metal cars, little packs of balsa wood, bottles of dandelion and burdock and bizarre confections which were fizzy or sticky and largely composed of additives. These were sold from huge jars kept on the shelf behind the newsagent's head. The shop assistant would pick them out by hand and, if you bought enough of them, pop them into a small, white, paper bag. Otherwise he or she handed them to you and you put them into your pocket to pick up a little fluff.

Comics contained many pages of uninterrupted type with authors such as Charles Hamilton (who as Frank Richards was the inventor of Greyfriars School, Billy Bunter et al) producing endless, long stories for both boys and girls. And the strip cartoons were well written and educational (both in terms of style and life). If you doubt me, just take a look at a child's comic from the 1950s and compare it with a modern comic. Those few children's comics which remain are brash and require little in the way of literary skills.

Playground fights involved fists and feet and were always widely advertised by shouts of 'Fight' for several minutes before they started. Spectators would gather around in a wide circle, giving the protagonists plenty of room to punch, kick, bite, gouge and pull hair. These fights were rarely, if ever, halted by a teacher, they never led to anything more than a nosebleed and they usually cleared the air between the protagonists. Proper battles involved small stones fired from home-made catapults, metal tipped arrows fired from home-made bows and bullets fired from air rifles and air guns. The number of children requiring plasters and dowsing with antiseptic was probably higher but the number of children requiring hospitalisation was far smaller than it is today. Most of the diseases from which children suffer today had not been discovered and so no one suffered from them.

Not all hobbies were as deadly as battles with catapults and bows and arrows. One summer, when I was around six or seven, I started to collect car numbers. It seems a strange thing to do now but there weren't many cars around in the early 1950s and car number plates were easily identified with the town where they were issued. A couple of pals and I kept notebooks in which we wrote down all the car numbers we could find. I gave up when my parents took me out for the day and parked in a crowded car park. I was overwhelmed and took to collecting stamps instead.

There were still plenty of working horses around and my father would go out into the middle of a main road with the garden shovel (the big one with built up edges which he used for clearing the snow which fell every winter) and collect the droppings left by the horses. I would stand and hold the bucket, unworried by the traffic or the idea that someone might see me. The manure was good for the roses in our front garden. That was the same garden where I cut the grass with a push mower. It took all my strength to move the mower if the grass was more than half an inch high but it was a privilege not a duty for I felt very grown up and it makes me now appreciate having a mower with a petrol engine which devours grass whatever the length.

When I was small, we lived in a prefab; a prefabricated building designed to ease the post-war housing crisis. I remember it as being quite well made. Each prefab had its own garden, complete with a wooden fence and a garden gate. I went back a few decades later and found that the prefabs had all been knocked down and replaced by a 20 storey block of flats. I had a look around and was astonished to see that the prefabs had been better built, sturdier than the new apartments, and they had those little gardens. The high rise flats looked gloomy; dirty, dark and depressing.

It was an innocent time in many ways.

And here's another odd thing I've noticed.

Back in the 1950s and as recently as the 1970s, children were still children but at some point they metamorphosed, sometimes overnight, into grown-ups. It was not a gradual process. Take a look at photographs of school children and then look at the team photographs for professional football or cricket teams from the 1970s and you'll see what I mean. Sports players in their late teens or early twenties looked like adults. And, by and large, they behaved like adults, too.

Today, children aren't children in the sense that they were half a century ago (there are a variety of reasons for this, which I have explored in other books) but nor do they metamorphose into adults when they reach a point in their lives when adulthood might seem appropriate. Grown men and women in their 20s and even 30s still look and behave like children. Just think of the way modern professional sports players behave if you don't believe me.

Young people born in the last decade of the 20th century and the first two decades of the 21st think that they are experiencing rapid change as social media changes daily but in truth they aren't experiencing anything like the change which their parents and grandparents had to face. All that is happening today is that life is becoming more complicated and technology is ever more intrusive.

My parents had no radio, no television, no telephone, and a motorbike with a sidecar was an incredible luxury. Motor cars were only for the very rich. My Dad made a television set in the kitchen of our prefab and, when Queen Elizabeth was crowned Queen, our living room was packed with people who came in to watch because we were the only people anyone knew who had a set on which to watch it. Our set had a screen that was smaller than a modern laptop screen. There was only one TV channel and that only operated for a few hours a day. (When I say that my Dad made our first television set I mean exactly that. He bought a magazine which contained instructions and then purchased the valves, knobs and bits and pieces from a local shop.)

Traffic wardens hadn't been invented and anyone who'd been on an aeroplane was probably either a business executive or an adventurer. Families who wanted to explore the continent travelled by train and boat or put their car onto the ferry; both provided a rewardingly slow and gentle introduction to foreign parts. Central heating was unusual and computers were as big as a grand piano and took half a day to struggle to add two and two. There was much whirring and crossing of fingers before the answer was spewed out.

You might imagine that all the technology we have at our disposal these days would have dramatically improved our productivity (in the widest sense of the word).

But it hasn't.

Despite the lack of technology, people in general always seemed to manage to get a lot more done before computers became widespread.

How many modern authors, pecking away at their laptops, can ever hope to match the output of Charles Dickens who wrote with a quill pen and died at the age of 58 – an age at which most modern writers would consider that they were just getting into their stride? How many can match the output of Mark Twain? And, remember, Frank Richards used to write 10,000 words a day on an old sit up and beg typewriter. (How his fingers must have hurt.) P.G.Wodehouse turned out a whole library of books on an old Royal desktop machine which was so big that I doubt if he could lift it without help.

How many modern film stars now make as many films as James Stewart or John Wayne?

Technology has slowed us down and it has certainly had a damaging effect on every aspect of productivity. The intrusive telephone started the rot. And today we are obsessed with our emails and, for those who choose to play that game, with the relentless, hourly demands of social media.

Things started to change in the 1970s but villages like Bilbury were still hanging on to a simpler way of life.

Even by the end of the 1970s, not all homes in Bilbury were supplied with electricity, mains water or mains drainage. In the big cities, it was commonplace to find houses which had gas supplied by pipe but in Bilbury, in the 1970s, anyone who wanted gas had to buy it in bottles which were collected from the local shop or, for a small extra fee, delivered to their door. Heating and cooking were mostly done with wood and, occasionally, with coal.

In towns and cities, most people had telephones, and television sets and washing machines and dishwashers: technology had tiptoed into the world and was, generally speaking, made very welcome.

In rural areas, however, things did not move quite so quickly. Even by the 1970s, there were a good many houses in villages such as Bilbury which were without telephones or television sets, and though a few homes had wireless sets, the equipment they had was large, cumbersome and reliable. I remember too that they all had a setting for something called Hilversum. No one knew where or what it was.

Every decent sized town had a department store, usually family owned and family run, where you could buy furniture, bed linen, crockery, clothing for all the family, sensible underwear (including iron clad corsets with straps strong enough to dangle a carthorse), hats and haberdashery. And, of course, every town had a Woolworths store; these were always fun to explore and full of colourful and useless joys – the perfect shops for children of all ages but absurdly over- stocked. At one point, Woolworths carried over 50 different types of pencil case. Woolworths was a store where people bought what they wanted rather than the stuff they needed. It was a store for the spur of the moment purchase but at least everything cost pennies.

In Bilbury, we had Peter Marshall's shop and though there were stores in Barnstaple selling things most of us could manage perfectly well without, it was to Peter's well-stocked emporium that most of us headed when we needed something.

As recently as the 1970s, many motor cars still smelt of leather and petrol instead of plastic and diesel, and if bits fell off (which they did from time to time) they could be fitted back into place by anyone who owned a wrench and a screwdriver. Cars were owned only by the rich and the ambitious middle classes and seat belts had not been invented. Windscreens were made of the sort of glass which splinters into sharp shards. Car owners expected vehicles to last for decades and even someone without skills or tools could replace a windscreen wiper or a broken wing mirror. Most car owners tinkered with their vehicles on Sunday mornings, sometimes removing the entire engine and working on it after lovingly placing it on the kitchen table. Washing and polishing the car was, for many enthusiasts, merely the end of the process rather than the process itself.

Back in the 1950s, drivers had regularly broken their wrists starting their cars with the handle provided but by the 1970s, cars were equipped with self-starters. A device called the choke, which had to be pulled out prior to starting the car on a cold morning and then pushed back into position when the car had begun to operate, had pretty well disappeared too. In the 1950s, a foot operated pedal dipped the headlights and if the car was posh, another foot operated the pedal oiled the chassis at 100 mile intervals. By the 1970s, cars no longer had bits which needed oiling quite so regularly and they didn't have a chassis either. But in Bilbury, most local people still drove vehicles which had been built in the 1950s and the local garage knew more about starting handles than cars without gear sticks. My first car, a Humber, was held together with sticky tape and bits of wire.

Despite all the dangers, it was safe to walk through the streets after dark and in small, rural communities, people really did leave doors and windows open without worrying that they would be burgled.

So, that was the 1970s – the time of which I write: The Bilbury Years.

Welcome, to those who remember some of this, and welcome too, to those who think I must have come from another planet and that the world I describe must be imaginary.

People used to say that things were better 'then' and when the 'then' was 100 years ago everyone knew it was nonsense. Things were only better in Victorian and Edwardian times if you were rich and had good, strong teeth.

But thinking about it as objectively as is possible, I do think things were better 'then' if 'then' was just half a century ago.

Back in the 1970s, we had anaesthesia, antiseptics and antibiotics (antibiotic resistant bugs were unknown) and roads you could drive on with a reasonable expectation of getting where you were going before the seasons changed. Women wore frocks and dresses and skirts and hardly ever owned a pair of trousers and men wore hats and took them off when greeting people. On buses, men would offer their seats to women without being abused. Obesity was far less common and infant mortality rates had fallen dramatically. Life expectancy was much the same in the 1970s as it is now though women generally lived a few years longer.

This difference is fading fast as women acquire bad habits such as smoking, and drinking and overeating which were previously almost exclusively male. The wider availability of household gadgets powered by electricity means that women take less natural exercise and the women's liberation movement has helped to ensure that the killer stress is shared more equally between the two sexes.

There is, by the way, a popular myth, sustained and promoted some who don't understand and by some who have a vested inte in selling the idea, that doctors and drug companies have together been responsible for conquering disease and improving life expectancy. But it is a myth that life expectancy has increased dramatically in the last hundred years and another myth that any improvement is a result of doctors becoming wiser and drug companies producing better drugs. What most observers do not realise is that when historians say that life expectancy was around 45 in the year 1900, they don't mean that most adults died at or around the age of 45. The figures are skewed by the fact that lots of babies died at birth or in infancy. Those tragic, early deaths dragged down the average life expectation. If a baby dies when it is a few months old and a woman dies at 90 then the average age of death is 45 years. Infant mortality rates have dropped dramatically and so average life expectancy appears to have risen dramatically.

What doctors and drug companies won't tell you is that infant mortality rates did not fall because of vaccines or drugs – they fell because communities separated their sewage from their drinking water, because overcrowded tenements were pulled down and because better farming methods meant that healthier, cheaper food became available. It isn't difficult to argue that doctors and drug companies have carefully and deliberately built their reputations on a well-sustained myth.

I have rambled enough.

I sincerely hope you enjoy this trip back to the 1970s and this latest collection of Bilbury memories.

Vernon Coleman
Bilbury, Devon, England

Boris and Belinda Bickerson

That variety of medical treatments sometimes rather patronisingly dismissed as 'alternative therapies' have, of course, been around for far longer than orthodox medicine. For many centuries what we now call 'alternative' or 'complementary' remedies were the only forms of treatment available.

Only in the last century or two have ordinary people been able to consult trained and qualified doctors, or expect to be looked after by nurses who have been given formal training.

Back in the 19th century, and before, the absence of properly qualified practitioners meant that communities everywhere, but perhaps particularly those in rural areas, were looked after by a wide variety of individuals who had some knowledge, or claimed to have some knowledge, about remedies which might be used to combat illness.

Some of the remedies which were used relied heavily upon the power of the healer's personality and upon the effectiveness of the placebo effect.

Other treatments, the secrets of which were sometimes passed down through the generations, usually from mother to daughter, relied on herbs – many of which were extremely effective.

The drug digitalis, still one of the most powerful remedies used in the treatment of heart disease, was first used by 'wise women', 'mydwyfes' and 'witches' who obtained the herb from the foxglove plant. It was only when an observant doctor noted the efficacy of the remedy, that digitalis was introduced into burgeoning mainstream medicine. There are hundreds of powerful medicines which come from plants – aspirin comes from the willow tree and morphine from the opium poppy. And, of course, penicillin is a lowly mould – penicillium – which had been used for centuries before being 'discovered' by Alexander Fleming in 1928. It is perfectly true that it was Fleming whose research, serendipity and observational skills helped turn the mould into a powerful drug for the treatment of infection but what many people still don't know is that penicillin was known and used by the ancient Egyptians. They used rotten bread in several remedies for the treatment of infected wounds and although they did not have laboratories in which to investigate and define the nature of the treatment they were using, they had the imagination to take advantage of the healing properties of the mould itself. It would be millennia before Fleming gave the mould a name and a scientifically approved purpose. The Egyptians also used scopolamine from the mandrake plant, cathartics from the castor oil plant and painkillers from the opium plant.

I doubt if there is any substance known to man which has not at some point been tried and used as a remedy for illnesses. Some of the substances which have been tried have proved ineffective, some have turned out to do more harm than good, sometimes even killing rather curing, but many have turned out to be effective and safe enough to be used.

I have, in my time, met a wide variety of healers.

Some, sadly, were charlatans.

For example, I once met a woman who claimed she could cure cancer with little rubber bands. If you had cancer of the lung, she put the rubber band on the little finger of your left hand. If you had breast cancer, she put a green rubber band on the ring finger of your right hand. If you had brain cancer, she put a red rubber band on the index finger of your left hand and a blue rubber band on your thumb. And so it went on. Gullible and desperate patients gave her money to tell them where to put the rubber bands and even paid her more for supplies of the appropriately coloured bands. (Naturally, ordinary rubber bands did not work as well as the expensive ones which she sold.) She had absolutely no medical training and no knowledge of human anatomy or physiology but she earned large sums of money by selling her 'cure' to vulnerable patients. When she died in 1971, she left her astonished relatives a fortune and a large, comfortable house in a fashionable London suburb.

It is, of course, possible to argue that even the most outrageous charlatan can do good if they are charismatic enough and if they clearly believe in the remedy they are promoting. The effectiveness of the placebo response has been well documented and it has been shown many times that a doctor who convinces his patients that the remedies he is offering will be beneficial will cure far more effectively than the doctor who simply tosses a prescription across the desk with a desultory, and rather disinterested: 'try these, they might help'.

The big, unanswered and unanswerable question, is: 'Is it better that someone should hobble about in pain, untreated and untreatable by orthodox physicians or that they should be given some relief by an unqualified quack?'

The problem is that there is no doubt that charlatans and quacks who know little or nothing about the human body and mind and who do not understand their own strengths and limitations, can do an enormous amount of harm.

The main danger, of course, is that by promising much and delivering little or nothing, the greedy charlatan may discourage the genuinely sick from seeking advice which could prove thoroughly advantageous.

(Incidentally, those who practise quackery are often accused of doing what they do for money but how many expensive practitioners, working in luxurious Harley Street consulting rooms, fail to provide their patients with a bill after treating them? And how many GPs do what they do without expecting to see money appearing in their bank account?)

I once saw a patient who was visiting North Devon on holiday and who had been 'treated' for nine months by a ruthless, money-grabbing quack in Bristol.

I was called to see the patient when he collapsed while driving on the road between Blackmoor Gate and South Molton. It was a miracle none of his passengers was seriously hurt for, when he was suddenly taken ill, he unavoidably drove off the road and into a ditch.

The man was emaciated and jaundiced, and I was astonished that he had managed to drive down from Bristol. The man's wife told me that her husband had a long-standing fear of doctors and of hospitals and had been treated by a local quack who had diagnosed constipation and had promised to cure him with a cocktail of liquid paraffin and senakot together with two hourly doses of methyl cellulose. I was called by a passing farmer and when I got to the scene of the accident, I was just in time to watch him die.

The autopsy showed that the unfortunate fellow had cancer of the kidney which had metastasised and, as a result, he had secondary deposits in just about every organ of his body. His liver was swollen, solid and lumpy.

It may not have been possible to cure the man but he would have most certainly received better medical and nursing care, and he would have had a much better chance of surviving, if the self-appointed 'expert' treating him had managed to put his hubris to one side, accept that his diagnosis and treatment might be wrong and find the courage to ask for help.

It was inevitable that there should be several practitioners of alternative medicine working in the North Devon area where my practice was situated. Most of them practised their versions of medicine as a hobby and all of those who I came across were, I'm pleased to say, as conscious of their limitations as they were of their strengths.

(My sister-in-law, Adrienne, had given up her own ministrations after various unfortunate attempts at healing. She had once taken a three day course in iridology which had proved rather less than successful and when I first arrived in Bilbury she was a keen practitioner of herbalism. She abandoned the herbalism after poisoning her father with hawthorn tablets. Her attempts to persuade Anne Thwaites to deal with the pain of childbirth with extract of nettles had proved equally unsuccessful.)

Some of the local practitioners were complete amateurs (not in the sense that they were unprofessional in the way they worked but in the sense that they neither asked for nor accepted any monetary reward). And some specialised and offered only remedies for particular conditions.

So, for example, a local farmer called Mr Hornbeam had a cure for ringworm which was quite remarkable. He simply drew a circle around the ringworm with his finger and within a week the skin would be clear and there would be no sign left of the problem. Mr Hornbeam was a man of few words and he could appear brusque. He was certainly not a man who could ever be accused of dilly dallying, shilly shallying or any other variety of prevarication. He was a man of action, a man who could comfortably be described as a doer not a thinker, but his treatment for ringworm was remarkably effective. I have absolutely no idea how or why it worked but work it certainly did.

Then there was Gilbert Carmody of Barbrook who had a very strange and curiously effective remedy for indigestion, particularly when caused by over-indulgence. He would, with the aid of his wife Hetty and his two huge sons, dig a man-sized hole in the largest manure heap on their farm. I saw the family at work on this task and I have to say that Hetty did as much work as the three men.

To say that Hetty was a big woman would be like saying that Mount Everest was a trifle on the hilly side. She was reputed to start each day with two kippers and a tumbler of green chartreuse and to end it with two more kippers and another tumbler of green chartreuse. She ate the kippers, bones and all, as a sandwich, positioned between two pikelets and always followed the kippers with a Chorley cake. I did once see her having her early morning kipper sandwiches and her tumbler of green chartreuse (and it was a large tumbler, the sort more normally used for serving lemonade) but although I never saw her finish the day with the same menu, I have no reason to disbelieve the tale. I have often come across strange dietary habits and I subsequently found out that Horatio Bottomley, the journalist, businessman and orator, used to start his day with kippers and champagne, but Hetty's preference still seems to me to take the biscuit, and to be well on the odd side of unusual.

Hetty's brother was a clergyman in Wakefield who was quite famous in ecclesiastical circles for having constant rows with his Bishop and who was more widely renowned for having written and self-published an apparently rather indiscreet tell-all autobiography entitled *Altar Ego*. His book, which Hetty said was extensive, revealing and rambling, was subtitled *A Candid Look behind the Vestry Door*. It quickly went out of print (I always suspected that the Bishop bought all the copies and burnt them) and Hetty promised to find me a copy but, sadly, never could.

Gilbert was quite a religious man whose favourite saying was: 'As a tree falls so it must lie'. He managed to make this biblical saying sound deeply enigmatic and apparently he used to say it whenever an indigestion sufferer disappeared into the manure heap. Mr Carmody would encourage the groaning sufferer to climb naked into the hole that had been prepared and the sons would shift and compress the manure so that the patient was buried in it up to his neck. Hetty, who had done much of the hole digging, took no part in the burying process. The sons were built along the lines of rather plain Corinthian pillars. This bizarre treatment produced a cure within a day and I can only assume that the heat of the manure heap promoted digestion. In the early days, they used to provide this service at no cost but in later years their remedy became so popular that they used to charge £2 per person. Their remedy was a little more expensive than a bottle of antacid, and required a good deal of bathing afterwards, but it seemed to work just as well.

I have certainly heard it said on several occasions that a hot bath is the best remedy for digestive troubles and a steaming manure heap would probably work on much the same principle.

It was a hell of a cure, though and I think I would have had to have pretty awful digestion before agreeing to climb into the depths of one of Mr Carmody's manure heaps. I often wondered if Mrs Carmody ever needed to take the manure heap remedy as a result of her unusual diet, but I never dared to ask. They were, to say the least, a forbidding family and the sons, who were very, very large, were rather humourless and easily offended.

Although they were really some way outside my normal catchment area, the Carmody family were long-term patients of mine (they had been looked after by Dr Brownlow) and I once visited them in winter. Mrs Carmody had a kipper bone stuck in the back of her throat and, fortunately, I was able to remove it with a long pair of forceps. It was so cold in their house (a 19th century farmhouse that had been rebuilt, redesigned and added to so often that it looked as if it had been designed by two architects who hated each other and their client in equal measures) that I suggested, not entirely as a joke, that if they had anything they wanted warmed up they should put it into their fridge. The sons scowled and one of them had pointed out that they didn't have a refrigerator. Indeed, they had no mains electricity: just a small, petrol driven generator which fed a couple of lights in their barn. They did their cooking on an old Aga which they fed with wood and bits of rubbish.

Oliver Hudson, who lived on the Barnstaple road and whose mother's maiden name was also Hudson, was another local practitioner. He claimed to be able to cure mumps by leading the sufferer three times around a well in his garden. He always told his patients about his mother's maiden name though I was never quite sure whether this was because he felt it was significant or simply because it was a curiosity of which he was proud. When not curing mumps, Mr Hudson was an income tax inspector with very personal views about history. He once told me that the Great War had been fought after the King, the Kaiser, the Emperor of Austria and the President of France had a private meeting and decided there were too many people in the world and that a few million ought to be killed (or, presumably, culled) in an attempt to keep the numbers down. Mr Hudson also assured me that whenever faced with a dilemma of any kind he would always ask himself what Napoleon Bonaparte would have done. I always found this a rather strange way to seek a solution to any problem since from what I knew of Napoleon, he always solved every problem either by invading somewhere foreign or by putting another one of his relatives on a throne somewhere. I was never sure whether Mr Hudson consulted Napoleon Bonaparte when dealing with tax dilemmas but my own experience of the Inland Revenue convinced me that this was not an unlikely prospect – though as a taxpayer I would have been startled if I had been advised to deal with a tax issue by invading Russia.

And then there was Absalom Cadell, who specialised in treating acne. He was in his late fifties when I first met him but he looked much older. He lived in a very scruffy cottage near Tolstoy's garage and was a quietly spoken man who had once worked on the railways. He had retired after an accident which had left him not with any physical abnormality but with a morbid dread of a number of things – including leaves, blood and, for some unexplained reason, hats of any description. Everywhere he went he walked slowly, with his hands behind his back. He reminded me greatly of an earnest undertaker pacing steadily and respectfully behind a hearse containing the mortal remains of a valued customer and knowing himself to be in sight of relatives who knew that tipping the undertaker's men was the right and proper thing to do if the deceased was to ascend to heaven with the proper level of dignity.

Mr Cadell had very fixed views on a range of subjects. 'Man or woman's determination to adhere to their understanding of the obligations of humanity is their only inviolable and fundamental responsibility,' he insisted. 'All personal and social loyalties, duties and roles are built upon that determination.' I never really understood what he meant by this but it sounded impressive and he said it often and loudly.

'It is the free man's right, nay his duty, to resent authority and to do everything he can to undermine the conceit of those who enjoy the trappings of the power they claim on its behalf,' was another of his favourite sayings. I understood that one and could see the point.

He was, to say the least, an unusual man.

But he was undeniably a miracle worker when it came to treating acne – his sole speciality.

He would give each of his patients a bottle containing a colourless liquid which was characterised by the dark-red sediment lying at the bottom. The ingredients were kept quite secret. The bottle had to be shaken vigorously and although I never tasted it myself, the stuff was reputed to taste quite foul. Patients had to take a tablespoonful in water three times a day and they had to drink three bottles of the stuff. Mr Cadell did not charge a penny for his remedy but simply asked that the bottles be returned to him when empty. He would only dispense one bottle at a time, so to obtain the second bottle the patient had to take back the first bottle. The stuff was reputed to be so acidic that it would gradually eat away the spoon which was used to dispense it. But the truth is that Cadell's Potion, as it was known locally, worked better than any medicine I was able to prescribe at the time and those who took it all said that their acne had gone away leaving no scars. To this day, I have no idea what the mixture contained or where the recipe came from.

Apropos of absolutely nothing, Mr Cadell once showed me an asbestos jacket which his grandfather had bought in 1944. He apparently bought the jacket not, as you might have thought, to protect himself against incendiaries, but because he liked to smoke in bed and had a habit of falling asleep and setting fire to himself. The jacket looked immensely uncomfortable and given what we now know about the perils of asbestos, it was probably not the healthiest piece of clothing ever designed.

And then there was Wayne Wellard, the farrier with the dog called Kamir. Mr Wellard was the man to go to if you had sore or strained muscles and although he had received absolutely no training, he specialised in massage and could ease troubled muscles in just one visit. My mother-in-law, Mrs Kennet, had visited him on several occasions and she swore that he was more skilful and more effective than any physiotherapist. To his patients he was known as 'Mr Fingers'. Although he struggled to make ends meet, Mr Wellard never charged anyone for his services. He said that if he charged he wouldn't feel so good about what he did and that if he didn't feel so good about it then it wouldn't be so effective.

The best known, and undoubtedly the most successful, alternative practitioners in the Bilbury area of North Devon were the Bickersons – Belinda and Boris Bickerson. They both earned a modest living by charging small fees and they always referred patients to me if they felt they were unable to help. I always felt that we had a good relationship.

Belinda and Boris were not husband and wife, they were brother and sister and neither of them had ever married. There was no little sadness behind their situation. Belinda had been engaged to an American soldier who had fought in the Korean War. I cannot remember how on earth she had met him and, indeed, I may never have known. Tragically, he had died within a month of arriving in Korea. Since then she had shown no interest in marriage or, indeed, in beginning any sort of romantic relationship. Boris had remained entirely unattached until he was in his 30s and then he had become engaged to a girl who was ten years his junior. When the girl got cold feet, changed her mind and gave him back his ring, Boris had been heartbroken. He too had abandoned romance. 'I've tried that, it didn't work and I won't be trying it again,' he told me once and in his voice you could hear the sadness and the disappointment in his heart.

The pair lived together in the rambling old house where they had both been born. They had inherited a decent sum from their parents and although they had their small incomes from their work as alternative practitioners, the dividends from their investments had for years provided them with a small but regular income which pretty well made them independent. Their father, who had been a dentist with consulting rooms in Exeter, had been a keen investor and had, apparently, put together a portfolio of solid, blue chip investments which the Bickersons refused to change in any way. He had also left them shares in a company which had been set up by his own father to sell potted meats both in cans and in small jars. When I heard about the potted meat company, I was reminded of a character in Oscar Wilde's play *Lady Windermere's Fan* who says, rather patronisingly, about an Australian businessman: 'Mr Hopper's father made a great fortune by selling some kind of food in circular tins.'

The Bickerson potted meat company had, in its day, been enormously successful but sadly, for the young Bickersons, it had fallen by the wayside, through changing tastes and a failure to move with the times I suppose, and one or two of their father's investments had turned sour and the companies, destroyed by the hubris and greed of management, had expired. Despite this, the Bickersons retained great faith in their father's selections and they steadfastly refused to accept outside advice or to sell any of the remaining share holdings. And, to be fair, their investments seemed to enable them to maintain their modest lifestyle.

In their garden, the Bickersons had the tallest and oldest oak trees in Bilbury. Every autumn since Patsy and I had been looking after Cedric the pig, the Bickersons collected up all the acorns they could find and brought them round to Bilbury Grange in a sack. I'm not sure why it is but pigs certainly love acorns. You might have thought that with a pig being so large and an acorn being so small there wouldn't be much pleasure in scoffing a mouthful of acorns but you'd be wrong, and there is no doubt that for Cedric the fruit of the oak tree was one of the greatest delights available: a delicacy to be chewed, appreciated and savoured. I'm sure the Bickersons would have brought Cedric their acorns in any case, but they were keen to collect up every one they could find because they had half a dozen Exmoor ponies and, of course, for ponies acorns can be quite deadly.

At the time of which I am writing, Belinda was in her mid-fifties and Boris was a couple of years older. She was well-built and heavy-breasted and had the biggest bottom I've ever seen on a woman or, indeed, a man. You wouldn't want her sitting on any delicate 18th century furniture. He was tall and rather thin and wore his hair in a ponytail. They had a strong but volatile relationship which seemed to bounce between love and loathing. If they had been brothers you would have said they oscillated between a loving David and Jonathan propinquity and a toxic Caine and Abel relationship. Some of their disagreements were almost comical in a strange way. So, for example, Boris smoked and Belinda did not. 'I will be very annoyed if I die before you,' I once heard her shout at him. On another occasion, when he was ill with bronchitis, she told me, with tears in her eyes, that she knew she would not bear to be alive without him. I suspected that the truth lay somewhere between these two extremes and I had no doubt that they were as close and as interdependent as most married couples.

The two Bickersons practised quite different forms of alternative medicine.

Belinda was what would sometimes be called a healer, though she preferred to describe herself as having 'the gift' or holding 'the cure in her fingers'. She wasn't a 'midwife' (or mydwyfe) in the old-fashioned, traditional sense of the word; she wasn't a purveyor of old wives' tales; she wasn't a herbalist and she didn't practise any of the orthodox forms of unorthodox medicine. I had heard it said by some that she must have been the seventh daughter of a seventh daughter but I know from my knowledge of her family history that she wasn't that either.

Whatever it was that she did, patients from all over Devon, and further, visited her and paid her with whatever they could. Some patients paid her with a few eggs or a chicken. I know that one man paid her with several square yards of turf. A vet from South Molton, who could have easily paid her in cash, paid her by looking after her ponies. A couple from Taunton gave her a small motor car after she healed their daughter. The girl, who was suffering from severe neurological symptoms, had been seen by doctors in Bristol and London. None of them had been able to make a diagnosis. Belinda had spent an afternoon with the girl and the symptoms which had baffled the doctors had completely disappeared by the end of the day. The parents later gave an interview to a national newspaper and insisted that Belinda had not even touched their daughter, other than to kiss her on the forehead when the two first met and again when they parted. Belinda refused to speak to the reporter and Boris chased a photographer down their drive, throwing sticks and stones at his posh German motor car. The couple had tried to give Belinda a cheque but she wouldn't take it, saying that it was far too much money for an afternoon's work. And so, noticing that Belinda didn't have a motor car, they had arranged for a brand new Mini to be delivered. It was one of the estate models, decorated with real wood on the outside and it was fully taxed and insured and it sat unmoving in an empty barn because neither Belinda nor her brother could drive.

Belinda had been born at a good time.

If she had been born a few centuries earlier, she would have been put to death as a witch. They'd have put her on a ducking stool and submerged her in the village pond. If she had survived the experience, then they would have known that she was a witch and they would have built a huge bonfire and burned her to death. If she had drowned then they'd have known that she was innocent. Everyone in the village would have breathed a sigh of relief because they hadn't been living with a witch as a neighbour. Poor Belinda would, of course, have been dead either way.

If she'd born a couple of decades later, and lived in the 21st century, she would have doubtless been barred from practising her skills by legislation which demands that everyone be able to show the requisite pieces of paper before practising their chosen profession. She would, I suspect, have been investigated by the police, irritated by social workers and exposed by the media.

But in the 1970s she was not just tolerated; she was respected and admired.

Her brother, Boris, was a bonesetter. He was not, he insisted, an osteopath or a chiropractor. He was insistent about that for, he pointed out, osteopaths and chiropractors are trained and have qualifications and he had neither. He was a bonesetter in the old traditional sense of the word and in a way, I suppose he too was lucky that he was born when he was. If he had been born thirty or forty years later he would have doubtless been hounded out of business by a society controlled by professional associations, civil servants and bureaucrats; a society which frowns on anyone claiming to have healing skills but not having the necessary certificates and paperwork.

As a child, Boris used to smash up rabbit skeletons with a hammer and then put them back together like a jigsaw. By his mid-teens, he could set bones. A girl in the village had a motor cycle accident and her ankle and lower leg were shattered. Several hospitals did their best but the bones were so badly broken that they told her she would always walk with a limp and never dance or run. The young bonesetter, who was still at school, turned up, uninvited and asked if he could help. He didn't say another word but just touched the girl's ankle and gently manipulated the bones. He visited every day for a fortnight and the mother, naturally sceptical and doubtless suspicious, sat and watched. In two months, the girl was walking normally. In four months, she was dancing.

How do you explain it?

I cannot.

But there are many things in this world which I cannot explain and just because I am unable to explain something it doesn't mean that it isn't happening.

Like his sister, Boris did not have a formal practice. He did not have a formal list of fees. But patients came to see him from miles away and he always saw anyone who turned up. He once had a patient, a boy in his early twenties, who had been brought down from Scotland by his parents. The parents had heard of Boris's skills through a relative who lived in the seaside resort of Ilfracombe. The three members of the family stayed in the Duck and Puddle for a fortnight. When they arrived, the boy had a terrible limp. When they left, he was walking normally. Gilly Parsons, the pub's landlady, told me that when the trio left, the parents both had tears of joy rolling down their cheeks. It was rumoured that a patient, a solitary man in his 40s, had travelled from Germany especially for a consultation but I did not see him myself.

Occasionally, a reporter would turn up and ask Belinda and Boris for an interview. A television crew turned up once too. But the brother and sister would never speak to anyone about what they did. This was not particularly out of a sense of modesty or a fear that they would be besieged by more patients than they could deal with. Belinda told me once that they did not like talking about their gifts because they were given to them by God. 'It would be disrespectful for us to take credit for our gifts,' she said. They both believed that if they gave interviews and talked about their work then God would take away the gifts He had given them. 'The people who need us will find us,' said Boris, quite simply.

The Bickersons had both enjoyed good health until one day when I had had a telephone call from Belinda asking me to call round to see her brother. She told me that he had a terrible pain in his right temple and double vision in the eye on that side. When I questioned her, she admitted that he also had difficulty opening his mouth.

I'd never seen a patient with the problem before but even before I saw him I was pretty sure that Boris was suffering from a disorder called temporal arteritis; a problem also known as giant-cell arteritis.

It's a disease that usually attacks older people, most commonly those in their 60s and 70s, and it affects more women than men. But in medicine, statistics are of limited relevance and even though a problem may be commoner in a particular age or ethnic group that doesn't mean that it cannot affect others outside the usual range.

When I arrived at their home, I realised that it was the first time I'd ever been inside the house. I knew them both well and we always stopped and spoke when we met in the village but they didn't mix socially with anyone in the village and I don't think either of them had ever been in the Bilbury village pub, the 'Duck and Puddle'.

Belinda took me upstairs. As we climbed the staircase, I couldn't help noticing that it was decorated on each side with beautifully framed prints by Hogarth which looked to me to be very early and probably very valuable. I wondered if they were original, prints actually made by Hogarth and his wife from the famous copper plates, and I couldn't help wondering if Patchy Fogg, my friend the antiques dealer, had ever seen them or even knew the prints were there.

'I can't do anything for him myself,' Belinda told me, as we climbed. 'I'm too close to him.'

Boris was lying in a huge four poster bed and he looked as ill and miserable as anyone would look if they had a bad headache and double vision and couldn't open their mouth properly. Actually, to be fair, he looked much more cheerful than I would have looked in those circumstances.

He had a slight temperature, the skin on his forehead and scalp was tender to the touch and he had double vision. When I talked to him, it was clear that he also had symptoms of polymyalgia rheumatica – a disorder which often goes hand in hand with temporal arteritis. He had severe pains in his shoulders and his pelvis which had started only that day. There was absolutely no doubt about the diagnosis. In large hospitals in London and in other big cities, temporal arteritis was being confirmed by taking a biopsy of the artery. I didn't think that would be available locally and I knew Boris wouldn't want to travel to the hospital. Besides, a negative biopsy result doesn't mean that the patient doesn't have the disease.

The treatment for temporal arteritis and polymyalgia rheumatica was the same then as it is now: quite high doses of corticosteroid. I took some blood to send off to the laboratory in Barnstaple and told

Boris that I would come back with some tablets I wanted him to take. I explained that the corticosteroid would need to be taken in quite high doses to start with and then gradually tapered off over the period of a year or maybe even a little more.

'Do you mean he has to take these pills for a year!' said Belinda, horrified.

'I'm afraid so. If he doesn't take them then the eye problem could get worse – and maybe even end up with Boris losing the sight in that eye.'

'But Boris hates pills,' said Belinda. 'And so do I!'

'I do too,' I told her. 'I wouldn't prescribe anything that wasn't essential.'

Belinda looked at me and then nodded.

As I turned to go, I noticed a cream silk nightdress neatly folded on the other pillow. I said nothing but headed back down the stairs followed by Belinda.

'It's just for the comforting,' she said, as I prepared to leave.

I looked at her, slightly puzzled.

'I saw you notice my nightdress,' she said. 'I forgot to move it.'

I put my arm around her shoulder. 'It's none of my business, nor anyone else's for that matter,' I told her softly.

She looked up at me and sort of half smiled. 'It's just for the comforting,' she repeated softly in an explanation I did not ask for or expect.

Incest happens a good deal in North Devon, especially in the more remote villages where in-breeding was common, but it was the first time I had come across it in Bilbury. If incest it really was. Maybe, as Belinda said, it was just for the comforting. But why should I interfere? I knew that Miss Bickerson had a hysterectomy many years earlier and so there wasn't any chance of there being any notable consequences even if they went a step or two beyond 'the comforting'.

I told her that I would be back with Boris's pills within twenty minutes or so, and that I would send the blood sample off to the laboratory in Barnstaple so that the diagnosis could be confirmed.

For the next month or so, Boris's condition improved steadily.

The laboratory confirmed that the diagnosis was the correct one and the corticosteroids I had prescribed did their job well. After a month or so, all of Boris's symptoms either disappeared or were dramatically reduced and the pains in his shoulders and other big muscles had completely disappeared.

And that is when the trouble started.

Patients are often unwilling to carry on with a course of treatment when the symptoms and signs of their illness improve.

'I talked to a friend of mine about these steroids you're giving Boris,' said Belinda one day. 'And she said these drugs have a lot of nasty side effects.' She pulled a piece of paper out of the pocket of the ancient cardigan she invariably wore. 'I wrote down some of the side effects,' she said.

'I know about the side effects,' I said gently. 'But the drug is curing Boris's condition.'

'High blood pressure, weight gain, cataracts, glaucoma, a swollen face, insomnia, nervousness, osteoporosis, stomach bleeding, swollen ankles, muscle weakness, increased chance of developing an infection…' Belinda read out a list of the known side effects.

'All that's true,' I agreed, interrupting the recitation. 'That's one of the reasons why I call in to see Boris every week. I want to see that he's still improving but I also want to look for any side effects. It's dangerous and irresponsible to give steroids to someone who doesn't really need them but when a patient has a serious disorder there is no doubt that steroids can be life-saving.'

'And the dose Boris is taking is very high,' said Belinda, who seemed to give more credence to what her friend had told her than to what I was trying to explain.

To be honest, I was not surprised by her attitude.

Belinda was proud and protective and apprehensive and not a woman who felt entirely at home in the latter part of the twentieth century. They did not have central heating, a modern stove, a washing machine or a television set. They cut their grass with a scythe and a strange-looking Victorian lawn mower which was pulled by one of their horses. She was, I think it is fair to say, nervous about anything invented since electricity and the telephone. Actually, I'm not sure that she was happy about either of those.

I tried to explain to her that I agreed with her that doing nothing is sometimes the best and safest option. 'There is a tendency these days for everyone to want to do something when the best results are often obtained by doing nothing – but doing nothing with a judicious mixture of caution, understanding and awareness – with a pinch of fear thrown in to keep everyone on their toes. But in Boris's case doing nothing would be dangerous and possibly fatal.'

I could tell by the way she looked at me that she still didn't believe me or accept that her brother needed treatment.

'The dose has come down dramatically,' I told her. 'And over the next twelve months I'll slowly taper the dosage until he can stop taking them.'

'Twelve months!' cried Belinda.

'I'm reducing the dosage already,' I told her. 'And it will come down a good deal over the next few months.'

But I could tell that Belinda wasn't happy.

When I returned a week later they were both unusually quiet and although Boris was still improving I knew that something was wrong.

'We've stopped the pills,' Belinda announced suddenly.

'We're very grateful to you,' said Boris. 'But I'm better now. My symptoms have all gone and there really doesn't seem any point in my still taking the drugs.'

I had been half expecting this.

As I have already pointed out, patients who feel well often don't want to take the medicines which they need. So, for example, patients who have high blood pressure may have no symptoms at all. They often wonder why it is necessary for them to take drugs. And if the drugs cause unpleasant side effects, as they often do, then patients may simply stop taking them with disastrous results. Patients with diabetes sometimes have very few symptoms and wonder why they need to carry on with their treatment. It is easy to persuade a patient who is in severe pain to take a painkiller but it can be difficult to persuade a patient who has a hidden infection to take an antibiotic which they need and which may cause nasty side effects.

'The symptoms went very quickly,' said Belinda. 'The drugs are very powerful and there is no doubt that they worked.'

Boris seemed embarrassed. 'But it seems silly to take the risk of continuing with them,' he said.

'You really do need to keep taking the steroids,' I told him. 'There's a lot the experts still don't know about temporal arteritis but the inflammation that caused your symptoms is probably still there and there could be a risk of it coming back.'

32

'Well if it does come back then I can start taking the tablets again,' said Boris firmly, as though this settled the question.

'It's not that simple,' I told him. 'For one thing the inflammation can affect a number of arteries in different parts of the body. If the condition flares up again you could lose your sight permanently.'

'Oh, I don't think so!' said Boris. 'I only had double vision last time. And the corticosteroids soon dealt with that.'

'I can't promise it would be that easy to deal with another time,' I pointed out. 'If we don't deal with this problem it could make you blind. And I don't know what's happening to your other arteries.'

I explained that the inflammation which had caused his earlier symptoms could affect arteries elsewhere in his body. 'There's even a risk that your aorta could be involved,' I said. 'And if your aorta becomes affected then the consequences could be terrible.'

'What sort of terrible?' asked Boris.

'An aortic aneurysm can develop,' I pointed out. 'The aorta is the biggest and most important artery in your body. If it develops an aneurysm then the aneurysm could burst. Or you could have a split or a tear in the wall of the aorta – a dissecting aorta.'

'Is that bad?' asked Boris, now a little quieter.

'It's very bad,' I told him. I saw no point in trying to hide things from him. I felt it was vital that he kept taking the corticosteroid tablets. 'If the wall of the aorta splits then blood can flow into the split and the whole aorta can rupture.'

'Can they treat that?'

'If the rupture isn't too big and you're close to a good hospital when the aorta splits, and there is no delay in getting you into the operating theatre and there is a skilled, experienced surgeon available to repair the split then it can be treated,' I said. 'That's rather a lot of 'ifs'.'

'My friend Matilda says that steroids are very dangerous drugs,' said Belinda suddenly. She'd been listening to what I had told them but she didn't seem to have heard anything I'd said. Maybe she just didn't want to hear what I'd told them.

'Is Matilda the friend who gave you the list of side effects associated with the steroids?'

'Yes. She has several medical books which she bought from her doctor when he retired.'

'Is she a doctor?'

'Not exactly a doctor, no.'

'A pharmacist?'

'No, she's a herbalist,' said Belinda defiantly.

'You know that I have great respect for all forms of medicine,' I told her, trying to remain patient. 'And I know that herbalists can help a lot of people. You must also know that I don't prescribe drugs unless I really think they're necessary!'

Both Boris and Belinda looked a little sheepish.

'You have to trust me when I tell you that the corticosteroids are necessary,' I said. 'I know it's difficult to believe that they're necessary now that Boris's symptoms have more or less disappeared but if you stop them then the consequences could be disastrous.' I agreed that steroids are powerful drugs which can cause a good many side effects, agreed that they obviously need to be treated with great respect but pointed out that when they are really needed there is no doubt that they can be life-changing.

'I don't believe in over-treating patients,' I told them. 'I don't treat patients when they don't need it or when they won't benefit from them. I do believe in trying to assess the risks against the gains. So, I wouldn't give a potentially lethal drug to a patient suffering from hay fever. The disease doesn't justify the risk. And I don't believe in recommending treatments which aren't sensible. So, for example, I wouldn't advocate an operation to treat varicose veins on a 97-year-old woman with heart failure, kidney failure, liver failure and septicaemia. But giving steroids to a patient with this condition isn't over-treatment. There are risks, of course there are risks, but the risks of taking the drug are much lower than the risks of not taking the drug.'

Boris and Belinda said they would think about it and Belinda said she wanted to talk to her friend the herbalist before making a decision. They said they'd come and see me in the surgery and tell me their decision. I asked if they would speak to a consultant in Barnstaple but they both refused.

It was three days before they came to a morning surgery at Bilbury Grange, and I knew the minute they walked into my consulting room that they had decided that Boris would not be taking any more of the steroid tablets.

I tried again to persuade them that it was important that he carried on with the drug. But I'm afraid I failed. I think Boris would have taken the corticosteroids if he had been alone. But Belinda, advised by Matilda, her friend the herbalist, was adamant that he should stop taking them.

And there was nothing more that I could do.

I suggested again that they speak to another doctor. I offered to make an appointment for them to see a consultant in Barnstaple or Exeter. I offered to speak to their friend Matilda to try to change her mind and to explain to her just how dangerous untreated temporal arteritis can be. But nothing worked. They were adamant. All that was left was for me to say a silent prayer that Boris would not suffer a relapse. I felt that it was not really the way I wanted to practise medicine.

Prayer has its place in healthcare but I prefer to use it alongside other remedies or as a sole remedy when there is nothing else that can be done.

For a while, I thought Boris had got away with it.

Another three months went by and in that time, I saw them several times, occasionally individually and sometimes together. Boris didn't come to the surgery but I called in when I was passing their home.

'I'm fine, doctor,' said Boris with a big smile. 'I didn't need those pills of yours after all!'

'You have to admit that Matilda was right and you were wrong!' said Belinda. She said it as though she were teasing but I got the feeling that there was also an element of seriousness about what she was saying. She seemed to enjoy the fact that the orthodox trained doctor appeared to have wanted to prescribe a powerful drug unnecessarily.

I didn't say anything.

I was not convinced that they had been right to stop the pills. I was still desperately worried that the inflammation might still be affecting Boris's arteries. And I was still concerned lest he suddenly lost his sight or suffered a major crisis if his aorta started to split.

It was his aorta.

You never know when these things are going to happen.

In a small way Boris was lucky, I suppose.

The problem with an aortic dissection is that the symptoms are easily confused with the symptoms of other disorders.

Patients who have a dissecting aneurysm in their aorta may have severe chest pain, severe abdominal pain or severe back pain. They may be short of breath, they may have difficulty in walking or, they may have the symptoms of a stroke. And so a dissecting aneurysm can be mistaken for a heart attack, a severe chest infection, a back problem or a stroke. It isn't always easy to make the diagnosis.

But with Boris, I knew when I took the telephone call what was wrong with him.

It was three o'clock on a Sunday morning. There was no moon and it was pitch black outside. It was raining heavily. I consoled myself with the thought that it wasn't too cold outside and it wasn't snowing!

'It's about Boris,' said a voice I recognised instantly.

'What's happened?'

'He's got a pain in his back,' said Belinda. 'It came on suddenly.'

'Did he say what sort of pain?'

'He said it felt as though something was tearing open inside him.'

'Can he sit?' I asked.

'He's half sitting up in bed,' said Belinda. 'He's sweating and pale and he looks awful.'

I didn't need to ask any more questions. I told Belinda that I would be at their house as soon as I could.

'Get him ready for me to take him into Barnstaple,' I told her.

'Are you going to call an ambulance?' she asked.

'There isn't time,' I told her. 'I'll take him there in my car. You can come with us.'

As I climbed into my clothes, told Patsy where I was going and told her that I would have to take Boris into Barnstaple myself, because there wouldn't be time to wait for an ambulance to arrive. I found myself wondering why medical emergencies so often seem to take place at night when the weather is bad.

'Why don't I call the hospital?' asked Patsy. 'I could tell them what's happened and that you're on your way.'

I kissed her, told her she was brilliant and asked her to tell the duty house surgeon that I was bringing in a patient with a dissecting aortic aneurysm. 'They'll need to get a theatre ready,' I told her. 'Tell them it's a patient who has temporal arteritis so there's really no doubt about the diagnosis.'

When I got to the Bickersons', I didn't bother examining Boris. I didn't even take his blood pressure. I told Belinda to help me carry him down to the car and we lay him on the back seat. Belinda squeezed in alongside him. It was one of many times that I was grateful that I had a large car with room for a patient on the back seat.

It was, I think, the longest journey I've ever made. On the way there, the weather gods decided to add a little lighting and thunder to the mixture they'd already prepared and to turn the night into a fully-fledged, full-dress rehearsal for the Day of Judgement and the arrival of the Four Horsemen of the Apocalypse. If those gloomy future hours turn out to be anywhere near as full of flashes and bangs as were the thunderstorms which ravaged North Devon that night, we will all be in for a shocking surprise.

The road to Barnstaple twists and turns. It goes up and it goes down and there are scores of blind bends. Fortunately, at that time of night there is usually little traffic and with the storm in full spate, I managed to drive all the way to Barnstaple without seeing any other motorist. I was convinced that Boris wouldn't make it to the hospital. I could hear him groaning with the pain, and Belinda told me time and time again that he was in distress and looked very ill. All I could do was to tell her to comfort him and to use every ounce of her healing power to keep him alive until we reached Barnstaple.

We made it.

The house surgeon, bless him, had believed what Patsy had told him and was standing in the hospital doorway with two nurses, two porters and a trolley.

They helped me put Boris onto the trolley and then whisked him straight to the operating theatre where the surgical registrar and a team of nurses were already scrubbed and waiting.

The anaesthetist later told me that if we'd taken five minutes more for the journey, Boris would have definitely been dead. If I'd called an ambulance and waited for them to take him into Barnstaple, he would have been dead. And if Patsy hadn't thought to ring ahead and tell them that I was bringing in a patient with a dissecting aneurysm, he would have been dead. Once again, that is a lot of 'ifs'. I was so very grateful that the hospital had believed me and had accepted the diagnosis which Patsy had relayed to them.

It was nearly 5 a.m. when I got back to Bilbury Grange and fell into bed for a couple of hours sleep before another day started.

It's easy to criticise Belinda and her friend Matilda for insisting that Boris stop the corticosteroids but I understand why they felt that way.

I just wish I had been able to persuade them that the drugs were truly necessary.

Still, Boris survived and so the whole affair had a happy ending.

And when Boris came out of hospital some time later, I had no trouble in persuading him (or Belinda) that he should take the drugs which had been prescribed.

Iolanthe and Bertie in River Cottage

River Cottage remained empty for nearly a year after the delightful Miss Gwilliams died.

No one wanted to live there because it was so close to the river that the ground floor was either wet or under water for most of the winter months.

The owners, a rather naïve couple from London, had bought the cottage in the middle of a hot summer, thinking it would make a splendid (and rather cheap) holiday home. They had apparently not noticed the high water mark on the internal walls downstairs. When their carpets, television set and furniture had twice been ruined by the uninvited river water which had entered their home, they decided they'd had enough. They tried to sell the cottage and this time were naïve enough to hope to recover a good part of the price they had paid. They were, I suppose, hoping to find another couple of innocent buyers. It was never going to happen.

In despair, they had offered the cottage a peppercorn rent of £20 a year. Their only stipulation was that the person renting the cottage would be responsible for all the outgoings such as repairs and local taxes. A lovely lady called Miss Gwilliams had rented it, perfectly aware of the watery drawback, and had turned the place into a home on stilts. She lived upstairs and hardly bothered with the downstairs rooms.

And then, when she had died at the age of 92, the Londoners had made another attempt to find a buyer.

This time they had been far less ambitious in their asking price and they had managed to sell the property to a couple from Ilfracombe, a seaside resort just a few miles away, who wanted to get away from the busy excitement of a town with a population that was, at the time, close to 10,000 in the winter and double that in the summer holiday season.

The village of Bilbury, with a modest year-round population of around 600, seemed perfect.

And there was no doubt that, if you were prepared to accept that the downstairs was pretty well uninhabitable, River Cottage was a pretty good buy. The average price of a property in Bilbury in the mid-1970s had, like property prices elsewhere in England, begun to accelerate and was already around £10,000 to £12,000.

In contrast, the asking price for River Cottage was just £3,500.

This was, I suspect, considerably less than the previous owners had paid for it. But they were, I think, relieved to get rid of the cottage which was for them undoubtedly a constant reminder of their mistaken enthusiasm.

And for that now modest sum, the buyer received the cottage, the river bank and half a stretch of river (the boundary line of the property ended in the middle of the river), five acres of rather scruffy woodland, three acres of pastureland and an old two storey hay barn. The cottage, which was just over 100-years-old, was one of the newest properties in the village. The barn was a youngster; no more than sixty or seventy-years-old.

Neither the Londoners nor Miss Gwilliams had ever done anything with the barn. And I doubt if they had ever intended to do anything with it. Miss Gwilliams was quite happy with the accommodation provided by the cottage. The barn held no attractions for her. The London owners had not seen the barn as an asset but rather as an unsightly excrescence, cluttering up a small portion of their landscape.

But, neglected and unwanted as it had been, the barn was a solid structure, built out of good stone and with walls which were two or three feet thick. The roof appeared to have been fairly freshly supplied with new, red tiles. If you had to have a barn in your life then it was a good barn to have.

Like the cottage itself, the ground floor of the barn flooded when the weather was bad and the river running high but the top floor, tucked under its newly tiled roof, was dry and rather cosy. There were, it is true, a few families of woodworm munching away at the rafters but they not been greedy and they had left plenty of wood behind to help hold up the stuff above them. Someone, at some stage, had even put four skylights into the roof so that the area wasn't at all dark or gloomy.

The couple who had bought the cottage, the barn, half a stretch of river and everything that went with them, were Iolanthe and Bertie

Fielding. There are few secrets in North Devon and it was widely known that they had obtained it for the fairly bargain price of £2,750.

For several years, the Fieldings had paid a rent of £5 a month for a neat two bedroomed white-washed cottage with a decent sized garden and spectacular sea views. The rent was low because although the house had been on the market for three years, with an absurdly low asking price, there had been no takers.

Most people who buy houses like to think that their new home will pretty well stay where it is and won't move about much. One or two London buyers had shown interest, thinking that they had perhaps spotted the bargain of a lifetime, but when they saw that the two neighbouring cottages had already fallen down onto the rocks below, they quickly withdrew their offers and hot-footed it back to the big city where accommodation may not have such splendid views but can usually be relied upon to be where you left it when you arrive home from work in the evening.

All had gone well until one day when Bertie Fielding had come home from a hard day emptying septic tanks and found his beloved, Iolanthe, sitting in the kitchen looking out of a large hole where a wall had previously been quietly keeping out the weather. The wall was now scattered among the rocks and the surf some distance below.

Fortunately, all was not lost.

The extraordinarily low rent which they had been paying for their cliff top cottage meant that the Fieldings had been able to put away a little money into their joint savings account at the Barnstaple and Ilfracombe Building Society and so, in due course, when their own cottage became uninhabitable and River Cottage became available, they were able to make a substantial down payment on River Cottage. The manager of the Barnstaple and Ilfracombe Building Society, who regarded the Fieldings as good customers, had been happy to make up the shortfall.

It is always nice when serendipity does a nice couple a good turn and in this instant there is no doubt that serendipity had done its business in spades.

I don't think I have ever known a couple to be so delighted at having bought their own home. They didn't care that the downstairs got a little wet from time to time. All they cared about was the fact that the house was theirs. 'So, our damp patch is bigger than most people's damp patch!' said Iolanthe, who was an ebullient woman with a laugh that could crack plaster. The jest always produced a jolly response and Iolanthe, never one to resist a jolly response, repeated it on every available occasion.

And to those who argued that living in a damp house must be unhealthy, Iolanthe pointed out that the previous tenant, Miss Gwilliams, had been 92-years-old when she had died.

It was good to see River Cottage occupied again.

I saw it shortly after Miss Gwilliams died and it looked a very sad place; almost entirely empty, with nothing in it except an old-fashioned, black, bakelite landline telephone sitting on the floor like a large toad.

The Fieldings were unusual in a number of respects and the most obvious was, perhaps, their age difference.

When Bertie and Iolanthe married, she was 67-years-old and he was just 20. Bertie's parents, a phlegmatic pair who were, generally speaking, regarded as pretty well impossible to shock, were nevertheless slightly surprised to find that they were a quarter of a century younger than their daughter-in-law.

Iolanthe had what can safely be described as an interesting past. She had been a nun, a librarian, a chorus girl in a troupe of entertainers which worked the cruise ships in the Mediterranean and the Caribbean, and a belly dancer in what sounded like a rather seedy nightclub in Cairo where, I confess, I always rather suspected that dancing was only one of her responsibilities.

She was an optimistic woman. When she and Bertie became engaged, she came to see me to ask if I thought she was too old to start a family. Disappointed by my discouraging reply she founded the North Devon Belly Dancing Association and started teaching belly dancing on Wednesday evenings in the Kentisbury Village Hall. Several of my patients became enthusiastic members of Mrs Fielding's class. Adrienne Fogg, my sister-in-law and Patchy Fogg's wife, was a regular student too.

Iolanthe's husband, Bertie was definitely not a belly dancer. He was well equipped in the belly department but not known to be keen on forcing it to undulate in public.

Bertie drove and operated a tanker which emptied cess pits and septic tanks and he was widely known, with searing and cruel accuracy, as Bertie the Stink. If you met Bertie dressed in his Sunday best and reeking of aftershave, you would still know what he did for a living.

(At the time there were, in and around Bilbury, four Berties and to avoid confusion they were all known by a qualifying addition to their names. This practice was imported from Wales, which is only a few miles away from the North Devon coast, where approximately 90% of the male population are called either Evans or Davies. To help villagers identify one another, Mr Evans the butcher will be known as Evans the Butcher, Mr Evans the baker will be called Evans the Baker and Mr Evans the taxi driver will be known as Evans the Taxi. And so, the Bertie who once worked at the garden centre on the road to the village of Westward Ho! was still known was Bertie the Plant even though he left the garden centre some years previously to take up employment as a butcher's assistant and part-time fireman. The Bertie who had been pool champion at the Duck and Puddle for as long as anyone could remember was known as Bertie the Balls. And the Bertie who delivered buns and pies for a baker who had a shop in Combe Martin was known to everyone as Bertie the Pie. Our Bertie, however, was Bertie the Stink. It is no relevance whatsoever but I cannot help pointing out that there used to be a Welsh undertaker in South Molton who was known to everyone as 'Dai the Coffin' and a Welsh vicar in Howbury St Mary's whose Christian name was Evan. I was always amused by that for has there ever been a more appropriately named clergyman?)

Once they had purchased their property, and its accompanying appurtenances, its barn, land and half a river, the Fieldings set about turning their new purchases into a home to suit their requirements.

Iolanthe and Bertie put a false floor onto the large ground floor of the barn so that Iolanthe could run her belly dancing classes at home. This, they decided, would save them a goodly sum of money for it would mean that they had no need to rent the Kentisbury Village Hall. It would also enable Iolanthe to expand the size of the class since the new ground floor of the barn was considerably larger than the nearby Village Hall. The false floor was carefully designed to sit a few inches above the high water level of the river in winter.

Upstairs in the barn, Bertie began to build the trestle tables which would carry his model railway layout. He was a remarkably patient man. He knew that it would be some years before his dream would be finished. 'It's something to get my teeth into,' he explained. 'A proper, big project!'

Bertie did not actually have a model railway but ever since he'd seen a railway modelling magazine, he had dreamt of owning a scale model railway; complete with stations, sidings, mountain passes, tunnels and little people standing around on platforms and in fields. I once had a patient who had a wonderful model railway in the loft of his home. He used to run trains according to a time table and when he died his widow carried on making sure that the trains ran on time – darting up the stairs to the loft to make sure that the 4.35 p.m. passenger train from Paddington to Truro left bang on time. When she went on holiday, she recruited a friend to keep the trains running.

Since Iolanthe and Bertie had decided to use the barn as part of their home it was, perhaps, not surprising that one or the other of them came up with the idea of building a bridge between the two buildings at first floor level. The bridge was designed to enable them to pass from their cottage to the barn during the winter months without having to put on waders.

It was not, of course, the sort of covered bridge which department stores commonly use to connect various departments which are separated from each other by road. It wasn't even the sort of solid bridge which railway companies build to connect the Up platform with the Down platform.

It was, to be honest, more the sort of bridge that is seen on those television documentaries which describe the lifestyle of fairly primitive people living in mountain areas – the sort of people who regard themselves as well dressed when they are sporting a loin cloth and a few feathers. The bridge consisted of two pieces of thick rope which were at one end tied firmly to bolts drilled into the cottage bedroom and at the other end to bolts fixed to the first floor of the barn. The two ropes were fixed about three feet apart, with one above the other, and to pass from one building to the other you walked along the lower rope, effectively a tightrope, while using the second rope as something to hold onto.

Both Bertie and Iolanthe were surprisingly nimble at crossing from the cottage to the barn, and vice versa, by means of their home-made bridge. I tried it once and twice and have to confess that I did not feel entirely comfortable doing so. These days, of course, planning officers, health and safety busybodies and regulation watchers or one sort or another would have put their feet down firmly and would doubtless have outlawed the scheme. The 1970s, particularly the 1970s as enjoyed in Bilbury, were a little less encumbered by such outposts of officialdom.

Iolanthe and Bertie had been living at River Cottage for about three months when Iolanthe came to see me complaining of what seemed a rather confusing collection of symptoms.

'I've got a terribly irritating cough,' she told me. 'And I've got a headache that just won't go away.

She was wheezing too, and clearly short of breath.

'I feel weak and I sweat a lot at night,' she continued. 'And I've got aches and pains everywhere. It's not like me.'

And it was not, I knew, at all like her.

Iolanthe Fielding may have been in her 70s but she was remarkably fit. All that belly dancing had kept her lithe and healthy.

'How is your appetite?'

'Gone. I used to eat like a horse. But now I hardly touch my meals.'

Put together, the symptoms rather reminded me of farmer's lung, a disease that wasn't particularly rare in my part of the world but seemed rather unlikely since Iolanthe wasn't a farmer and never had been. I checked her pulmonary function with a small gadget I had purchased after seeing an advertisement in the back of a medical journal. The reading I obtained proved what I already knew – that Iolanthe's breathing was poor. I then took some blood samples and sent her off to the hospital to have her chest X-rayed. It seemed possible that she had asthma or a chest infection – maybe even pneumonia. If it hadn't been October I'd have even considered the possibility that she had hay fever. But October is definitely not the hay fever season in North Devon. I wasn't convinced that Iolanthe had an infection so I didn't start her on antibiotics.

And then the next day Bertie came to the surgery with exactly the same symptoms.

'I don't know what Iolanthe's got,' he said. 'But I've caught it. The darned thing must be catching.'

And for a moment I thought perhaps it might be a chest infection after all. I took some blood from Bertie and sent him along for a chest X-ray.

I seriously considered starting them both on antibiotics but, and I don't know why, I was still convinced that they had some sort of allergy problem rather than an infection.

I tentatively made the diagnosis the following day when Mrs Pearce, a local spiritualist whose claim to fame in the village was that she had the most extensive collection of cacti in North Devon, came into my surgery complaining of pretty much the same symptoms as Iolanthe and Bertie.

And the bells started to ring deafeningly loudly when Adrienne Fogg came in complaining that she too was short of breath, sweating and had a cough and a headache.

I then realised that, unlikely as it had seemed, my first diagnosis had been the right one.

None of them was a farmer but they all had farmer's lung.

Now, farmer's lung doesn't sound terribly threatening.

It appears, at first, to be in the same category as housemaid's knee or tennis player's elbow – an unpleasant disorder that produces symptoms which are usually temporary and not too difficult to treat.

But farmer's lung is a terrible disease and very threatening. It's a horrid disease. It is also known as hypersensitivity pneumonitis and, like all diseases with an – 'itis' at the end of its name, it is an inflammation. In this case, it is the lungs which are inflamed.

Farmer's lung is an allergic disease which is caused by inhaling mould spores which lie in the dust of old hay, straw or grain.

In the same way that plants produce seeds, so moulds produce tiny spores. These are so tiny that around a quarter of a million could sit comfortably on a pin without fear of being overcrowded. The mould spores become attached to air born dust particles and wander about in the air. It is, therefore, easy for anyone in an area contaminated by mould spores to inhale three quarters of a million in a minute. And so someone who spent an hour in a mould-contaminated area could easily end up inhaling around 50 million spores. That's a lot of mould spores.

Normally, the body gets rid of dust particles and spores by sneezing or coughing. But mould spores are inhaled in huge numbers and they are very small so there is a real risk that a good many of them will get through the body's defences.

When they do manage to travel into the body, the spores settle into the lower part of the lungs and produce toxins which travel into the bloodstream. The body's reaction to the toxins produced by the spores cause permanent damage to the lungs and that's why the patient finds it increasingly difficult to breathe. The whole reaction of the body is a huge allergy reaction which produces symptoms rather like pneumonia. However, the condition is not in the slightest bit infectious or contagious. The only reason that several people may all suffer from the condition together is that they have been living or working together in a contaminated area.

The acute form of farmer's lung tends to develop quite quickly after exposure to the mould spores – usually within a day or two at the most. The symptoms may then hang on for a week or two.

The problem becomes serious when the patient is repeatedly exposed to mould spores. And then the symptoms just get worse. Farmer's lung can often become chronic, causing damage to the lungs and leading to serious long-term consequences. Eventually, the disease is irreversible and sufferers have increasing shortness of breath. They become exhausted by any exertion, they are physically weak and they cough pretty much constantly. It is a very, very unpleasant disorder. A good many farmers have lived out their final years incapacitated and unable to do anything other than sit in an armchair.

The cause of the problem was obvious, of course.

I hurried round to River Cottage and found both Iolanthe and Bertie sitting upstairs in their small living room. They were in a bad way.

'You stay here,' I told them. 'Do you mind if I have a look around your barn?'

They obviously didn't mind.

Not fancying their rope bridge (which I had tried and found a little too exciting for my taste) I went downstairs and across the short distance to the barn.

The barn appeared to have been cleaned – both downstairs and upstairs – but when I managed to crawl underneath the false floor which had been installed downstairs for Iolanthe's belly dancing classes I found that there were huge amounts of old hay and straw under the new floor boards. Iolanthe and Bertie had never bothered to clean out that part of the barn, assuming, I suppose, that no one would ever see that it was rather untidy.

Now I knew why they and some of their students had farmer's lung.

I went back to the cottage and told them both that they were not to go into the barn for the time being. I told Iolanthe that her classes had be cancelled for a while and I told Bertie that he would have to put his model railway on hold until the barn had been properly cleaned.

I then got in touch with Adrienne and Mrs Peace and other members of the belly dancing class.

Fortunately, none of them had developed severe symptoms and it was clear that within a week or so they would all make a complete recovery.

My own symptoms, which developed the evening of the day when I'd crawled under the false floor in the barn, included nasal congestion, itchy eyes and a nasty skin rash. Thankfully, all those annoying symptoms disappeared within 48 hours. I was lucky: I didn't get any of the breathing problems. But that may have been because I had the knowledge and the foresight to wear a dust mask when I went into the barn.

Iolanthe and Bertie wanted to put on masks and to clean the old hay and straw out of the barn themselves but I persuaded them that this would not be a good idea. Instead, they brought in a specialist firm from Taunton. Men wearing decontamination suits went under the false floor with huge, powerful vacuum cleaners and removed all the bits of hay and straw and all the old dust. It wasn't cheap but it was the most efficient way to clean the barn and make it safe for everyone.

Until this had been done, the barn was closed to everyone.

It took a little while, but everyone made a full recovery and when Bertie, Iolanthe and the belly dancers went back into the barn, there were no further problems.

Within a month, the River Cottage barn was full of life.

Downstairs, Iolanthe and her ladies were busy cramming themselves into suitably uplifting bras and Middle Eastern looking skirts on which they had sewn lots of sequins. Several of the dancers, including Adrienne Fogg, fixed fake rubies into their belly buttons. (Adrienne used a rather strong glue to fix hers and it remained there for two weeks before it fell out when she was in the bank in Barnstaple.)

And upstairs, on the first floor of the barn, Bertie and his father (whose name was also Bertie) were busy building what promised to be the foundations for the largest model railway layout North Devon had ever seen. They had not yet bought any trains or any track, let alone those wonderful little model railway porters and passengers which always help to make a model railway look lived in, but they had made good progress with the tables upon which the whole structure would depend and they had built the backboards upon which the diorama would be painted.

For Iolanthe and for Bertie, business at River Cottage was back to normal.

Dear Miss Gwilliams, a gloriously lively lady, had been very happy in River Cottage and she would, I felt sure, have been delighted to see how much fun Iolanthe and Bertie were having in their new home.

The Celebrity

At first I couldn't remember who he was or, indeed, if I knew him at all. If I did know him then I couldn't remember his name or where I had met him.

I smiled at him and took his outstretched hand.

Patients, even temporary ones from outside the village, don't usually want to shake hands. They come in, sit down and tell me what's worrying them. That's the way the ritual works.

But he definitely wasn't a patient of mine and I knew he didn't live in Bilbury. The population of Bilbury was, at the time, no more than 600 or so and I knew everyone in the village by sight and by name.

That was one part of the puzzle solved.

I was also pretty sure that he didn't live anywhere else in North Devon.

I'm not sure why I knew that but people who live in the wilds of North Devon are somehow distinguishable from visitors from the rest of the world.

Even the resident incomers who have moved into North Devon from other parts of the country, and who have retained their own regional accents are, after a while, fairly easy to identify as 'locals'.

I couldn't tell you why.

Maybe it's the windburn on their faces and hands.

Or maybe it's the slightly relaxed way they meander through life.

'You're looking very well!' the stranger said, when he'd let go of my hand and had sat down. He had a very limp, rather moist handshake and a suntan that had either been obtained from repeated trips to the Caribbean or from long hours lying on a sunbed. He was wearing a rather posh pair of aviator glasses which, I suspected, had probably cost more than the total cost of everything I was wearing. He didn't remove them. He was also wearing a stunningly unconvincing hairpiece which sat on the top of his head like a small, furry animal with its nose tucked under its tail. His waist had gone to

50

the same place as his hair and in its place there was a bulge that would have looked startling on a woman who was carrying triplets and about to deliver them.

'You too,' I said, playing for time and desperately racking my brain in the hope that my inbuilt computer would throw up a name to match the face.

The thing was that his face and voice were both familiar but I wasn't sure whether I really did know him or if he was perhaps someone famous whom I knew only from films or the television. When we meet people we have watched a good deal on the screen, it is natural to think that we know them – and that they must necessarily know us too.

His cheery manner and friendly smile rather convinced me that I did actually know him.

I obviously did not know him well but maybe I had met him somewhere. Maybe, I thought, he was someone I had met when I was making television programmes; a minor celebrity, perhaps: an actor, a television 'personality' or some such. Maybe he and I had chatted in the green room while waiting to go on a television chat show. I used to do the rounds of such things when I did book promotional tours: a radio chat show in the morning, a newspaper interview at lunchtime, a television news programme in the afternoon, a chat show in the evening and a late night radio talk programme to round off the day. A day in day out routine which for me never lasted more than two or three weeks, thank heavens, but for actors, promoting films could go on for long, tiring months. I once met the actor Simon Ward when he had been on the road for six months promoting a film called *Young Winston*. How anyone could cope with answering the same questions for six months was quite beyond my ken.

My patient had the tired, forced and slightly overeager smile of the minor celebrity who knows that if he is not to disappoint then he must constantly sparkle, and that if he is to rise up the ladder of show biz success then he must always be on show, always willing to do whatever it takes to gain another fan, another admirer.

In my experience, such individuals manage to convince themselves that every glance is a glance of certain recognition. When they go out into the world they pretend to do so in disguise so that they aren't photographed by the paparazzi, but the disguise is

51

never difficult to penetrate and they are always disappointed (and sometimes rather cross) if they go to an 'opening' or a fashionable restaurant and no one bothers them.

There is, in practice, only a relatively small divide between the minor and major celebrity and it is a gap which is invariably crossed only as a result of the whims and tyrannies of fate. To the struggling would-be star, the gap must sometimes seem at the same time both tantalisingly small and depressingly unbridgeable. When I made television programmes, I always felt slightly sorry for those who were desperate for fame; so desperate that they would, if necessary, readily accept notoriety as an acceptable alternative and, hopefully, a stepping stone to glory. Most were, in my experience, far more interested in fame than they were in riches.

(One friend of mine, a radio presenter, once confessed that his only aim in life was to be recognised in the supermarket and that he would do pretty well anything to achieve that ambition. But would he have been happy? It's a moot point. Maybe he was lucky not to achieve his ambition for if he had succeeded then he would have doubtless discovered the disappointments, frustrations and fears which are an inevitable part of being a star, and there is a chance that he would have been just as unhappy but without the hope to keep his spirit warm.)

But the fact that the new patient had spoken to me as though we were acquainted, seemed to confirm that we really had met and that he wasn't just someone I'd seen on the television or a magazine cover.

'I'd heard you'd tucked yourself in the wilds of Devon!' he said. 'Lost to the world and hidden away in a tumble-down mansion with your beautiful wife and a host of favoured animals. It's been said that you've abandoned us all so that you can minister to the local sick and needy; a veritable Dr Schweitzer with your own little cottage hospital. That's what I hear.'

'It's hardly a mansion,' I said. 'Though I agree it is rather tumble-down; in parts at any rate.'

'You live a long way from anywhere, don't you?'

'Not really. We're here and this is where we want to be, so we're not a long way from anywhere that we want to be.'

'I got my Chief of Staff to find your address,' he said, as though finding me had been a monumental task. In reality, it wouldn't have taken a serious researcher to find me. I was, after all, listed in the local telephone directory.

'You have a Chief of Staff? That sounds very impressive!'

I really was impressed for I honestly thought that only American Presidents had a Chief of Staff.

'Oh yes,' he said. 'She's a sort of glorified personal assistant. But if you allow them to call themselves your Chief of Staff you can get away with paying much lower wages. They regard the title as status and the status is worth money – they think of themselves as having a foot in the door of show business.'

'Like washing the elephants?'

'Exactly! Or playing the rear half of a pantomime horse. You should get a Chief of Staff for yourself. Don't you get troubled with fan mail?'

I laughed. 'The last reader who contacted me got my name wrong. She wrote to my publisher saying 'I'm a big fan of Veronica Carter. I've read all her books about Bilbury.' So I don't think I need anyone to help me deal with the fans.'

'I was talking to Terry Wogan about you the other day. I asked if you'd died but he said you couldn't be because he'd seen in one of the papers that you'd written another book. I said that maybe you'd died but had left behind a cupboard full of manuscripts which were now being released one at a time to a desperate public. But here you are and I must say you don't look in the slightest bit moribund. Indeed, you look a lot younger than I remembered.'

'No,' I agreed. 'I'm pretty sure that I'm not dead yet.'

'Are you still writing those books of yours?' he asked. 'And are you still writing for the newspapers? I haven't seen your by-line recently.'

'I'm still writing,' I said. 'But these days I don't write for newspapers or magazines. I just write books.'

'One thing I must tell you,' he said, not terribly interested in my answer, 'I came out here yesterday, just to check out the lie of the land, and I called into your local pub for a pie and a pint.'

'The Duck and Puddle?'

'That's the one.'

'An excellent pub; a proper village pub!'

'Brilliant pub,' he agreed. 'Wonderful pies. Marvellous beer. But the fellow behind the bar was the spitting image of that very famous celebrity psychiatrist Professor Eckersley. You must have heard of him?'

'Ah,' I replied, immediately. 'I'll tell 'Harry' the barman. I'm sure he'll be amused.'

I knew that Professor Eckersley didn't want people in London knowing that he was pumping pints in the Duck and Puddle under a nom-de-plume. He wasn't ashamed of his job. But, like Greta Garbo, he just wanted to be left alone.

'For a few minutes I thought it really was him. And then I thought about it and realised what a daft idea it was. Why would London's most famous psychiatrist be pulling pints in a pub in rural Devon?'

'Why, indeed?' I said.

'Must be a doppelganger.' He sounded rather disappointed.

"Harry' will be tickled pink,' I said. 'Is this Professor Eckersley famous?'

'Famous, my love? Oh he's famous all right! He treats all the film stars. He must be worth a fortune. I've met him several times myself.'

He said this as though he were scoring points and I realised that he was one of those very competitive people who seeks every opportunity to express superiority over others. At some point they usually say something like 'This isn't going to be a competition' in a tone which makes it clear that as far as they are concerned everything in the world is competitive.

I was reminded of a slyly competitive boy called Humphrey whom I knew at school.

'Your watch is fast,' I told him one day.

'Faster than yours?'

'Well, yes,' I replied, slightly puzzled.

Humphrey beamed. 'That means it must be better, doesn't it?'

There's really no way to deal with such people other than to agree with them and to express undiluted admiration.

'I'm impressed,' I told the stranger who, after purring for a moment or two, looked at me, holding his head on one side, and examined me as a bird might contemplate a prospective meal.

'You don't remember me, do you?' he said suddenly, rather sharply, on the edge of being offended.

'Of course I do!' I replied, offering a smile of recognition as a token of our apparent friendship.

It wasn't a proper fib because I knew I'd seen him somewhere. I just couldn't quite remember where or when or precisely who he was or what his name was.

'Do you remember making a television programme usually presented by Eamonn Andrews?' he asked, mentioning a programme which was broadcast on the television from London. 'It was only a few years ago,' he added.

And then I remembered.

'Of course,' I said. 'You interviewed me about *The Medicine Men.*'

The Medicine Men was my first book – it was a polemic about the over-close links between the medical profession and the drug industry.

'That's right!'

'You're Logan Berry!'

'That's me!' he agreed. He showed me a huge expanse of sparkling white teeth in what I am sure he believed was a smile. Sadly, the teeth were as convincing as his hair. They were sparkling plastic and designed to be seen from the back row of the circle, rather than from three feet away.

'I was the guest host for that programme. Eamonn was off somewhere else and they hired me as the stand-in.'

Logan Berry was not his real name, of course.

His real name, I remembered, was Percy Braunschweiger but like many celebrities he worked under a more memorable name. You can't become a star if your name is Percy Braunschweiger. I suspected that the name 'Logan Berry' had been selected by his agent or manager. When renaming a prospective star the aim is always to find a name short enough to fit on the front page of a tabloid newspaper. It helps enormously if the name is unusual enough to be memorable. And if the first name can be unique that helps because a newspaper sub editor can then put 'Logan' as a headline (as in 'Logan Eats Mouse for Bet' or 'Logan Spends Night in Nunnery') and everyone will know to whom it refers. If your first name is 'John' or 'David' this simply doesn't work for there are far too many Johns and Davids around.

Suddenly I remembered it all.

In fact, I remembered more than I wanted to remember about Logan Berry.

Meeting him had not been a particularly jolly experience and after our meeting I'd wanted to give him a black eye. Patsy had threatened worse, far worse and I seemed to remember that her threats had involved a pair of hedging shears and a garden hoe.

Logan, I remembered, was one of those people who earns a living on the fringes of show business and who acquires a sort of indistinct fame without having any definable or discernible skills. He couldn't juggle, do magic tricks or dance. He wasn't particularly good at telling jokes and he wasn't a very convincing actor. He couldn't write or play any musical instruments and he certainly couldn't sing. He didn't even have much charm.

What he did have, however, were a fake smile, which he could turn on and off like a light bulb, an ability to promote himself shamelessly, and a willingness to do anything a producer or an editor wanted him to do. Embarrassment was to him as alien as shame. He had, I seemed to remember, once spent a day lying in a bath full of baked beans. For a children's television programme he had sat in pretend stocks while children threw jelly and blancmange at him. In the pantomime season, he happily played an ugly sister or a cruel landlord. In the summer, he worked in theatres at the end of the pier where he made a fool of himself wearing outrageous costumes and merrily prancing about the stage. Offer him a cheque and an audience and he would do and say whatever you wanted him to do and say.

We had, as he reminded me, met on a television chat show.

I had been on tour promoting my first book.

Dr Brownlow had still been alive then and in those days it was not impossible for me to take some time off to promote my books. Logan, who had no medical training and as far as I know no skills or knowledge of anything other than himself, had been hired by the producer to present a programme on which I was booked to appear. One of Logan's tasks was to provide a review of my book live on air.

He had duly launched into a toxic attack in which he had argued that drug companies were doing life-saving work and that I, as a doctor, should be grateful to them rather than critical of some of their methods. He had pointed out that the British Medical Association did not approve of my book, or my criticisms of the drug industry or its influence on doctors. He had added spice to his review by suggesting that as a country GP I really didn't know what I was talking about, had got above myself and should go back to dealing with, as he so memorably put it: 'varicose veins and pimples'.

I had very little experience of television at that time and my attempt at a response was smothered with sneers and laughter from Logan and the programme's other guest and when I pointed out that I had done two year's research for the book, the pair of them dismissed this as irrelevant. I can't remember who the other guest had been. Logan then added that he had been told I had been struck off the medical register for unprofessional conduct and that I wasn't really entitled to call myself 'doctor'.

I was so astonished and horrified by this outrageous lie, a shocking libel, that for a moment I couldn't think of anything to say other than a bald and simple: 'That's not true!'. Logan, prompted in his ear by a message from a terrified studio director who was doubtless worried about lawyers and lawsuits, had immediately offered an ill-tempered apology but the damage had been done.

I remember that I left the studio feeling drained and with an empty feeling in the pit of my stomach.

And now the author of my pain was sitting in my consulting room in Bilbury.

'We had a lot of good fun with your book, didn't we?' said Logan. He frowned, as though in thought. 'Remind me: what was the book about?'

'You may have had good fun,' I said rather more coldly than I intended. 'I don't remember it as being particularly jolly.'

'Oh, you mustn't take these things personally!' Logan said dismissively. He waved his hand, in the casual manner of a man brushing away a cobweb.

I quietly counted to ten, picked up some paperclips and made a short chain. I hate it when people dismiss unfounded criticism as 'not personal'. How could I not take his attack personally? Any book written with heart and passion is a part of the author; as much a part of him as a leg or a kidney. Criticising a book and saying 'don't take it personally' is like criticising a new hairdo and saying 'don't take it personally'. Of course you're going to take it personally. It is personal.

I didn't say anything in reply and was quietly proud of my restraint. The man, though unwelcome, was in my consulting room as a patient.

'What can I do for you?' I asked him. I put the paperclip chain to one side. I was tempted to add: 'Is it varicose veins or pimples?', but I didn't.

'As I thought you would know,' he said, 'I'm appearing in a show in Barnstaple. I'm playing the Wicked Witch in a very wonderful production, and while I was in the area I thought I'd call in and ask you about a little something that's been worrying me.'

'But why come all the way out to Bilbury?' I asked him.

'I remembered you worked in the area and I thought you'd be the man to see,' said Logan, lowering his voice. 'I wanted to see someone I knew but not my usual chap in London. He can be very indiscreet. It's a very confidential problem and with you being in the business, as it were, you'll understand that we need to keep this under our hats.'

'In the business?'

'Show business, of course, dearie!'

'Ah.' I really didn't think of myself as being in show business though it was true that I had for a few years held an Equity card.

I wondered why on earth he had sought me out after being rude to me on the radio. And then I realised that he didn't think of himself as having been rude. To me it was an important subject, something worthy of serious debate, but to him it was just a knockabout few minutes on the wireless and a nice cheque from the broadcaster at the end of it.

'A boyfriend noticed it,' said Logan. He lowered his voice again. I could hardly hear what he was saying. 'It's a little something in a very delicate place,' he added.

Three minutes later he was lying on my couch, with his trousers neatly folded and hanging over the screen. His stomach was so huge that I had to ask him to hold it up out of the way while I examined the target area. Every inch of his skin appeared to be tanned.

'It's in the left one,' he said.

And it was.

There was a palpable swelling on the left side of his scrotum.

'Is it the big C?' asked Logan, hardly able to breathe.

'Do you get any pain with it?' I asked.

'Occasionally I do. Sometimes it's a sharp pain and sometimes it just aches.'

'Does anything make it worse?'

'It hurts most after a performance,' said Logan. 'I'm always very energetic on stage and we have matinees on Wednesdays and Saturdays. By the evening it really aches.'

'What about at night? Does it hurt at night?'

'No. It seems better when I lie down. Is it an infection? I'm very careful who I go to bed with but you never really know, do you?'

'It's a varicocele,' I told him.

'What on earth is that?' he demanded, sitting up with some difficulty. I wondered how on earth he managed to prance about on the stage. He really was very fat.

'It's like varicose veins inside your scrotum,' I explained.

'Not the big C?'

'No.'

'Not an infection?'

'Do you have any symptoms of an infection? A discharge from your penis? A rash anywhere? Urinary troubles?'

'Nothing at all except this silly lump. Actually the fellow who spotted it said he thought it might be worms living in there. I did a gig on the Isle of Wight last year and you never know what you can get when you go to foreign parts.'

'I don't think the Isle of Wight is foreign.'

'Well it might as well be. You have to go across to it on a ship.'

'A ferry.'

'Well I thought we were never going to get there. I'm not good on ships.'

'It's just swollen veins,' I told him. 'Not worms, not cancer and not syphilis or gonorrhoea.'

'Will it turn into anything else?'

'No,' I told him. 'It might get a little worse. It could affect your fertility.'

He laughed. 'Oh, I'm not bothered about that!' he said. He lay back again, gasping. He looked like a beached whale but he sounded like a fish out of water. He had obviously spent a lot of time sunbathing. The tan was so complete that I thought he had probably been using a sunbed.

'Do I need to have it removed?' he asked.

'Not unless it's causing you a lot of trouble,' I told him.

'Oh, not that much,' he said quickly. 'I try to keep away from surgeons whenever possible.' It appeared that the pain which came on the days when he did two shows was suddenly not quite so troublesome. I have found that this often happens. When a patient discovers that something they thought was serious is not, after all, either deadly or threatening, then the symptoms associated with it somehow become a little less troublesome.

I told him that he could get dressed and he started to pull up his underpants, which he had pushed down to his knees, instead of taking them off completely. They were boxer shorts covered with little pictures of ducks. As he pulled them up, I suddenly saw a small, dark patch on the outside of his left knee. It was about half an inch across, with irregular edges. The area around it was red, as though it were inflamed.

'How long have you had that?' I asked him, pointing to the patch on his skin. I had gone quite cold.

The moment I saw it I knew exactly what it was. Tests would need to be done. A histology report would be required. But there was really no need for any investigations. I knew exactly what I was looking at. There was, I thought, no little irony in the fact that Logan had come into my surgery worried about one problem when the real danger lay in another area entirely.

'Oh that's been there for years,' he said dismissively, pulling up his duck covered boxer shorts. 'It's probably been there all my life. It's just a mole thingy. I've got rather attached to it. Jeffrey calls it my beauty spot.'

'Jeffrey?'

'Jeffrey is my young friend, the one who found that wretched, little lump in my scrotum.'

I nodded. 'Has it changed at all?' I asked him.

'It may have got a bit bigger,' he said. 'I don't really notice it much.' He peered at it. 'The edges used to be round,' he said.

The edges were not now round; they were irregular.

'Does it itch?'

'Sometimes it does.'

'Does it ever bleed?'

'No, I don't think so. No, I'm pretty sure I've never seen any blood coming out of it.'

60

I looked at it closely and I could see a drop of bright red blood at one corner. Logan was so obese that he probably couldn't see his knees properly without making a real effort to do so.

'Do you use a sunbed?'

'Oh yes, I hate pasty white bodies,' he said. 'I usually go to a sunning parlour in London, one of the best, a very fashionable place, but I found one down here that works just as well.'

'I think you need to get that looked at,' I told him, trying not to alarm him too much. 'I want you to see a skin specialist.'

'Really?' said Logan, much more cheerful now that he knew that the lump in his scrotum was no more than a lump of varicose veins. He was clearly not in the slightest bit concerned about the skin problem I had spotted.

'Really,' I said.

'I'm not very bothered about it,' he said. 'I think of it as a sort of beauty spot,' he added again.

'It's something you should have looked at,' I insisted.

'Do you think it's something to worry about then?' he asked, starting to get off the couch.

'It's something that needs to be checked,' I told him.

I held out a hand, like a traffic policeman. 'Just stay on the couch for a moment or two.'

I then checked his groin, looking to see if any of his lymph nodes were swollen; to check if the cancer had spread. I got him to undress completely and checked around the rest of his body. I couldn't find any signs that the regional lymph nodes were affected.

'You've got me worried now, doctor,' said Logan. 'You're not playing with me because you're upset about that business in London, are you?'

'I' m not playing with you,' I told him, rather offended that he would even think that, but realising that Logan was such a malicious fellow, untethered by the restraints of good intentions, that he probably imagined everyone else to be the same. 'But you need to get that patch of skin checked out.'

I picked up the telephone, rang the hospital in Barnstaple and spoke to the dermatologist's secretary. She managed to fit Logan into an appointment in two days' time.

Logan, now rather more subdued than he had been on his arrival, left my surgery clutching the piece of paper on which I had written the date and time of his appointment and the name of the doctor he was due to see. I always tried to write such things down for patients. When you are worried it's easy to forget things you've been told or instructions you've been given.

'Will I need to see you again, doctor?' asked Logan, before he left.

'Probably not,' I said. 'The dermatologist at the hospital will look after you now. When do you go back to London?'

'The show has another fortnight to run.'

'Well, I've no doubt that the hospital in Barnstaple will write to your doctor with all the necessary details.'

'Thank you,' said Logan.

He looked at me and bit his lip. He clearly wanted to say something else. I waited.

'On reflection I think I was a bit unfair about your book,' he said.

I didn't say anything.

'I think I owe you an apology,' he continued. 'The producer told me to give you a hard time. I think someone gave him a few quid to make sure that you and your book got roughed up a bit.'

I nodded. I had guessed that he hadn't been rough on me of his own volition.

'But I was impressed with you,' he said. 'You seemed to me to be an honest doctor – someone I could trust. That's why I came to see you rather than just finding a doctor in Barnstaple.'

'Thank you,' I said. It meant a lot. We shook hands. And then put his hand into his inside jacket pocket and pulled out a piece of paper. He handed it to me. 'Take this with my compliments,' he said, as though he'd just handed me the deeds to Buckingham Palace.

When he'd gone I examined the piece of paper he'd given me. It was a ticket for the show he was in – just one ticket. I put it underneath my blotter. Two months later, I found it and threw it away.

I sat there for a few moments and thought about the vanity, the fear and, possibly, the sense of inadequacy which drives people to spend hours lying underneath a suntan lamp. Skin cancers are dramatically greater among individuals who desperately work on their tans. I realise that other people think very differently but it seems to me to be a potentially high price to pay for a relatively small benefit.

And it occurred to me, not for the first time, that vanity, fear and inadequacy have always been a significant cause of problems of many different kinds.

Many people start smoking because they want to look 'cool' and sophisticated. Others drink too much alcohol because they are frightened to say 'no' when drinking with friends in a pub. And some people, both men and women, have plastic surgery which they really don't need simply because they want to improve their attractiveness to others.

Vanity, in all its forms, can cause big problems. It has, throughout history, led to many a disaster. And Logan's vanity very nearly led to his death.

I never heard from Logan again but the dermatologist later told me that he was almost certain that Logan's melanoma (for the diagnosis was confirmed) had been triggered by the long hours he spent lying under a sunlamp. Sunlight, whether real or artificial, can cause an apparently harmless mole to turn nasty.

Luckily, the cancerous growth had not spread.

Logan's lymph nodes were not affected and after the patch of skin had been removed, his prognosis was excellent.

But if Logan had not come to my surgery because he'd met me in London and was worried about his harmless varicocele, and if I hadn't happened to notice the dark growth on his skin, then things could have been very different, and there is no doubt that the outcome would not have been anywhere near as successful.

Once again: so many 'ifs'.

Funny how things turn out, isn't it?

He Who Laughs Last

Unless you count the time when he came to help me deal with hungry wasps which had built a nest within the old walls of Bilbury Grange and were munching their way through my consulting room ceiling, I couldn't remember the last time I'd seen Thumper Robinson in my surgery.

'Sorry to bother you, doc,' said Thumper. 'But I've got a bit of a problem.'

'Tell me,' I said.

It was strange having to treat one of my best chums as a patient.

This is, of course, one of the drawbacks of practising in a small village. I knew all my patients well. Some were friends and some, like Thumper, were very close friends.

'My pee has turned blue,' he said bluntly.

My first thought was that the blue colouration must have been caused by something he had eaten. And the only food I knew of which caused urine to turn blue is turkey meat, which contains a substance called tryptophan.

'How blue is it?' I asked.

'Very blue,' replied Thumper.

'Do you have any other symptoms?'

'No. Just the blue pee.'

I gave him a small glass bottle and sent him out to the downstairs lavatory so that he could provide me with a specimen. A couple of minutes later he returned clutching a bottle of urine that was very definitely blue.

I asked him all the relevant questions such as 'Have you ever noticed this before?' and 'Have you eaten any unusual foods?'

The answers were all negative.

I was now becoming concerned. The only disease I could think of which can cause urine to turn strange colours, including blue, is porphyria. And porphyria, of course, is the disease which is believed to have been the cause of George III's madness. (As an aside, it was the king's madness which is reputed to have resulted in America becoming independent and breaking away from British rule.)

Trying not to show my concern, I then started to quiz Thumper about other symptoms which can occur in porphyria. He had none of them.

And, since porphyria is usually inherited, I asked him if anyone in his family had the disease. I didn't expect him to answer in the affirmative and he didn't.

Thumper wasn't at all keen but I insisted on taking a blood sample, which I put aside with the urine sample. I told Thumper that I would send them both off to the laboratory in Barnstaple.

Thumper thanked me but did not seem especially concerned. It occurred to me that he probably didn't realise just how dangerous porphyria could be.

Fifteen minutes later, I was astonished when Patchy Fogg came into the surgery.

'I thought I'd better come and see you because my urine has gone green,' he told me after we'd chatted about this and that for a couple of minutes.

He insisted that he hadn't eaten any unusual foods and that he wasn't taking any medicines that I didn't know about – even ones bought over the counter from a pharmacy. He had not, he said, eaten any asparagus for weeks. He said he knew that asparagus could make urine go green but he said he also knew it gave urine a funny smell and his urine didn't smell that way at all. He had no other symptoms at all. He had no stinging and no urinary frequency. Once again, I sent him out to the downstairs loo to fill a sample bottle with his urine. And when Patchy came back there was no mistaking it: his urine was green.

Now, there aren't many problems that can cause green urine and the only one I could think of is an infection caused by a pseudomonas bacteria. I told Patchy that I'd send the sample off to the laboratory and that as soon as I'd got the results I'd be in touch to tell him whether he needed any treatment – and if so, what. I also took a blood sample. Patchy clearly hadn't expected this and he wasn't very happy about it. But I insisted that it was necessary.

Twenty minutes after Patchy had left, I could hardly believe my eyes when Frank walked into my consulting room. He was, he said, the last patient of the morning surgery.

'Sorry to bother you, doc,' he said. 'But I've got a bit of a problem with my wee.'

I may not always be the brightest star in the firmament but even I was now beginning to suspect that something strange was going on.

'What's the problem with it?'

'It's gone orange,' he said.

My suspicions were now soaring high above the clouds.

Frank, like Thumper and Patchy had absolutely no symptoms of any kind. And he hadn't been eating anything unusual. Blackberries and rhubarb can cause the urine to change colour but he hadn't eaten either of those.

And since I prescribe all the drugs that Frank takes, I knew he wasn't taking any medicines that could cause his urine to turn orange. My first fear was that he had some sort of hepatitis. Infections of the liver can cause the urine to go orange and then dark. I checked Frank's sclera because they usually become discoloured in jaundice but they were fine.

And for the third time that morning I sent a patient out to the downstairs loo to pee into a little glass specimen bottle.

'I need a blood sample too,' I told him.

He seemed strangely reluctant. 'Oh, there's no need for that, doc,' he said, standing up and backing away.

'I need to send a sample to the laboratory,' I insisted.

'I'll come back tomorrow if it isn't any better,' he said, heading for the door.

'I'll get this off to the lab today,' I told him. 'But I really need a blood sample.'

But he'd gone.

I sat in the surgery for a while, wondering what on earth was going on. It was clearly quite impossible for my three friends to have all developed diseases which resulted in their urine changing colour.

And then two things happened which helped me to understand.

First, I looked at the calendar because I had to sign some letters which Miss Johnson had typed for me.

Second, Patsy came into the consulting room and told me that Thumper, Patchy and Frank were all standing around outside Bilbury Grange. In fact, she said, they weren't actually standing but, rather, they were leaning against the side of Thumper's truck. And, she added, they seemed to be very happy about something because they were all laughing their heads off.

'Do you know what the date is?' I asked her.

'Something towards the end of March? '

'Close,' I said.

I pointed to the calendar.

'Ah,' said Patsy.

'They're waiting until I go out to do the visits,' I said. 'Then they'll tell me that I've been April fooled. And they'll have a good laugh at my expense and tell me not to bother sending their urine and blood samples to the laboratory because there is nothing wrong with them.'

'The rotters!' laughed Patsy.

It was, of course, the first day in April. And the day on which, traditionally, people play jokes on one another. But it was still only 11.30 a.m. and there was plenty of time left for a little more entertainment. Traditionally, in England practical jokes can only be carried out before noon on April 1st so I had thirty minutes left in which to try to turn the tables on them.

I went out and feigned surprise at seeing my chums all standing around. Patsy came with me.

'April fool!' my three chums cried in unison.

They then explained that they had all eaten some food dye to change the colour of their urine.

'It was Harry's idea,' said Frank. He was referring to 'Harry' Stottle, the barman at the Duck and Puddle. 'Harry' Stottle's real name was Professor Eckersley and in a previous life he had been a professor of psychiatry and a fashionable Harley Street psychiatrist.

'He had a hunt around in Gilly's kitchen and found three dyes we could use,' said Patchy. 'We were going to come in all with the same coloured urine but 'Harry' thought you might think it was the water supply, telephone the Water Board and start a major panic.'

I congratulated them all on the gag and told them that they'd well and truly had me fooled. 'I expect you used a special non-toxic food dye, didn't you?' I said.

They looked at one another.

'What do you mean, a special non-toxic food dye?' asked Patchy. 'We used food dyes from the kitchen at the Duck and Puddle.'

"Harry' said we'd be fine in a day or so,' said Thumper. 'The dye is just excreted in the urine. It doesn't do any harm.'

'As long as you used a special non-toxic dye,' I said. 'The stuff which chefs and cooks use is toxic if you consume it raw. It only loses its toxicity when it's in something that's cooked at over 100 degrees Centigrade. But if you have enough of the stuff to produce a change in urine colour it can be pretty deadly.'

'What sort of toxicity?' asked Patchy who was not laughing any more. He wasn't even smiling.

'How deadly?' asked Frank earnestly.

'Is it dangerous?' asked Thumper.

All three of them were now very pale.

'It can very nasty,' I told them. 'The toxins used in the dye preparation are destroyed by heating but if you eat the stuff raw then the toxins will affect your livers and kidneys. It can produce necrotising relapsing hepatitis and long-lasting impotence. The only way to prevent the stuff causing permanent damage is to drink lots of water and flush the toxins out of your body. Oh, and you mustn't drink any alcohol for at least a month until your livers have recovered.'

'What sort of hepatitis?' asked Thumper, who was panicking. 'And how long-lasting is the long-lasting impotence?'

'How much water did you say we need to drink?' asked Frank.

'Two or three pints of water straight away,' I told him. 'That would probably be enough. There are some pint mugs in the cupboard next to the sink.'

The three of them rushed into Bilbury Grange, heading for the kitchen.

Patsy and I followed and found all three of them busily gulping down glasses of water from the tap. Thumper hates drinking water but he was swilling the stuff down as if it were his favourite beer. They drank at least three pints of water each.

'Do you think we'll be OK now?' asked Patchy, breathlessly. Water dripped from his chin. The three of them stood there exhausted, still holding their empty pint mugs.

I looked at my watch. It was one minute to twelve noon.

'You'll be fine now,' I said. 'But I'm afraid you'll spend most of the afternoon dashing to the loo.'

They looked at me. They'd noticed me checking my watch.

And suddenly the penny dropped.

'Food dyes aren't really toxic if they aren't cooked, are they?' asked Patchy quietly.

'I wouldn't think so,' I replied. Now it was my turn to grin.

'You've all just been April fooled!' said Patsy, smiling.

The three of them groaned.

'Do we really have to avoid alcohol for a month?' asked Thumper.

I shook my head.

'Thank heavens,' said Thumper, sounding very relieved. 'That was the scariest bit.'

Too Much of a Good Thing?

Donyard Hill is a transvestite.

His day time job is as the Secretary of the Kentisbury Golf Club but he has what would be called a secret if it weren't so widely known.

When he isn't chasing up members who have forgotten to pay their subscriptions, or who have broken on the club's many and constantly changing rules (the club committee even has a rule about the type of socks which male members can wear if they are wearing shorts), Donyard dresses in the sort of clothing usually worn by members of the opposite sex. He turns from Donyard into 'Molly', his alter ego. His gracile wife Cynthia-Anne helps do Molly's hair and make-up and seems to enjoy the whole experience just as much as Donyard himself.

Thumper, Patchy and I once had to rescue Donyard after he was arrested by the police for the great crime of walking around Barnstaple while wearing a frock. Since thousands of women do this every day without being arrested, or even worrying that they might be arrested, this seemed a trifle high handed to say the least. The three of us dressed up in some of Donyard's spare dresses, blouses and so on and drove to Barnstaple. When we got there, we told the police sergeant in charge that we were all on our way to a fancy dress party which was due to be attended by the Chief Constable. The sergeant, embarrassed and alarmed, duly released Donyard and apologised profusely.

Other than that unexpected and definitely unplanned hour or two of excitement, I had not seen Donyard very often. He and Cynthia-Anne tend to go into Exeter or Taunton for their adventures together and it is rare to see either of them in the Duck and Puddle.

He turned up at an evening surgery looking very different to how I'd seen him on the night of his arrest.

This time he was wearing a three piece tweed suit, a check shirt and a club tie that would not have gone well with any jacket or shirt but that presumably meant something to Donyard and to the people who had designed it.

'I've been a bit under the weather,' said Donyard.

I hadn't liked to mention it but he didn't look too good. Patients don't expect to walk into their doctor's surgery and hear him say: 'My word you do look poorly!'

Donyard had put on weight and he was showing some of the muscular rigidity associated with Parkinson's disease. He was also twitching and the muscles I could see all seemed to be going into and out of spasm.

He then suddenly closed his eyes, fainted, keeled over and fell off the chair.

I leapt up from my own chair and hurried round my desk but by the time I'd got to him, the fall had woken him.

'Golly,' he said. He looked around, as though confused. 'I don't feel too good,' he said. 'I've got this damned headache. I've had it for days. I simply can't get rid of it.'

I took off his jacket and his waistcoat and then helped him up onto my examination couch. Once he was lying down, I took off his tie and unbuttoned his shirt. Underneath his shirt he was wearing a very pretty corselette in lilac. There were lots of bows and a good many pieces of fancy lace. I also undid his belt and unfastened his trousers. Underneath those he was wearing a very fancy pair of lace edged panties in lilac silk. Stockings were attached to the straps on the bottom of the corselette, which was fancier than anything I'd ever seen before.

The truth is that folderols were not commonly worn in our part of the world.

Stockings were still the normal leg covering in Bilbury in the 1970s but only because they were available, normal and generally accepted as regular leg coverings. They were seen as functional rather than as exotic, special or sexy. Occasionally I saw women wearing pantyhose or tights but these were usually visitors from big cities such as London and Birmingham or tourists from America. Peter Marshall, our village shopkeeper, had tried selling tights for a while and had given up because there was simply no demand for them. Little did any of us know that within a year or two, stockings would be worn mainly by transvestites and bank robbers who pulled them over their heads to disguise their features (tights are just no good for robbing banks unless you work in very close pairs). Nor did we have any idea that women would soon be routinely wearing trousers and jeans – with surprisingly large numbers looking as though they were members of the Women's Land Army who had worked so hard on British farms during the First and Second World Wars.

Over the years I found that, as far as underwear was concerned, the ladies of Bilbury could be divided into three groups.

The ones under 30 years of age all held up their stockings with suspender belts. The ones between the ages of 30 and 60 generally held up their stockings with the aid of simple corsets or girdles fitted with suspender attachments. And the ones over the age of 60 generally wore corsets so complicated and robust that they took twenty minutes to remove and just as long to put back on again. The corsets favoured by this age group appeared windproof and probably bulletproof and were possibly stronger than some of the material used for modern house construction.

Only occasionally did I see patients wearing anything which could be described as lingerie, and any emporium selling flimsy folderols would have found life difficult in North Devon.

Donyard did not, of course, fit very neatly into the usual categories and his fancy underpinnings were, I gather, largely purchased on trips to the metropolis.

When I finally got down to skin, I couldn't help noticing that the Golf Club secretary had grown a very decent sized pair of breasts. They were not, perhaps, in the topless dancer category but they were of a very respectable size and seemed certainly large enough to impede his back swing, not to mention his follow through.

'Pretty damned good, eh?' said Donyard, who had now recovered from his collapse and who seemed enormously proud of his newly enhanced figure.

I definitely got the feeling that he had been waiting to see my reaction when his new breasts were uncovered. He was full of eager expectation; desperate to share his delight. He reminded me of a little boy with a new penknife or a little girl with a new doll.

It was clear to me that Donyard must have been taking a drug of some kind.

Gynaecomastia, the enlargement of the breasts in a male body, is not a particularly unusual occurrence but although it can occur in men who put on a good deal of weight and it can occur in some medical conditions, it is almost invariably a side effect of taking prescription drugs. There are quite a few medicines which can cause the male breast tissue to swell – sometimes to a quite appreciable extent. I had, over the years, seen quite a few men who had very decent sized breasts; mammary glands that would have delighted many a woman and would have certainly thrilled all those teenage girls who examine themselves each morning for signs that business in the chest area is booming.

'Remarkable!' I said drily. 'What have you been taking?'

Healthy men of his age don't usually grow breasts unless they develop a hormone imbalance resulting in the production of too much oestrogen and too little testosterone. Given the fact that Donyard was a crossdresser, I thought the most likely explanation was that he was taking something he should not have been taking.

'Aren't you going to congratulate me?'

'Congratulations,' I said drily.

'I'm a 38C,' said Donyard, proudly telling me his bra size. 'I reckon in another month I'll be a 38D.'

'What have you been taking?' I asked him again.

There was silence for a moment. 'I took some of my wife's birth control pills for a while,' confessed Donyard at last.

I remembered that Cynthia-Anne had come to see me one month with a strange and rather convoluted tale of having left her pack of birth control pills in her cardigan pocket and then having put the cardigan into the washing machine. She had a reason for putting the birth controls into her cardigan pocket but I can't remember what it was. I have found that when an explanation becomes too complicated it is probably fabricated.

'But she couldn't think of any other excuses for getting more pills,' said Donyard. He paused. 'And, to be frank, she felt bad about lying to you.'

He was still twitching. And although he was reasonably coherent he still seemed more than a little confused.

'So what have you been taking?'

I tried to remember what drugs can cause gynaecomastia. The list is surprisingly long. Anything which contains oestrogen will cause breast enlargement, of course, since one of oestrogen's main actions is to produce breast tissue growth. Quite a few antidepressants and tranquillisers can cause gynaecomastia. And so can steroids of various kinds. Amphetamine, heroin and marijuana can all cause breast growth.

'I got some pills from a Canadian magazine,' said Donyard suddenly. 'They were guaranteed to cause breast tissue growth.' He looked down at his chest. 'And damn me, they've worked haven't they?'

'Have you got the pills with you?'

'They're in my jacket pocket.'

I went over to his jacket.

'Left hand outside pocket.'

I reached into the left hand outside pocket. There was nothing in there but a comb and a penknife.

'Try the other one.'

I tried the other one and found a packet of pills. I looked at the side of the box. The name on the side of the box was Haloperidol.

I could hardly believe my eyes and I felt cold inside. Haloperidol is a powerful antipsychotic medicine which has dramatic actions on the brain. It is a drug which is used to treat schizophrenia. And it can cause a mass of side effects – including gynaecomastia.

I now understood why Donyard was twitching and had so many muscle spasms.

'How long have you been taking these?' I asked him.

'Six weeks or so.'

'How many have you been taking a day?'

'Three. They said you needed to take three a day for maximum effect.'

'Donyard, you're an idiot,' I told him.

I do not usually abuse my patients. But on this occasion it seemed entirely justified.

'Will they do me any harm?' he asked, suddenly worried. 'The magazine which sold them to me said they were perfectly safe and would just give me nice boobs.' He showed the mixed emotions of a man who has been told, on the same day, that he has just won the lottery but has only three weeks to live and enjoy it.

'They are not safe,' I told him. 'They can cause a lot of side effects. Breast enlargement is one of the least dangerous side effects. If you need to take them to deal with a serious health disorder then the side effects are probably acceptable. But you don't have anything wrong with you, you don't need to take them and so the side effects are definitely not acceptable.'

'I suppose you think I should stop them?'

I looked at him.

'You definitely think I should stop them.'

I glowered at him.

'I think I'd better stop them.'

I put the packet of pills I'd taken from him into a drawer in my desk.

'Will the twitching and confusion go away if I don't take the pills?'

'Yes, I hope so. But it may take a while.'

'I've been a bit stupid haven't I?'

'No.'

'No?'

'You've been a lot stupid.'

'Oh.'

'Unbelievably stupid.'

'Yes, I suppose I have,' he admitted. 'What will happen to my new breasts?'

'I don't know.'

'Can you ask someone? Or look it up in one of those big books in your bookcase?'

'No one can tell you. And no book can tell you.'

'Oh.'

'All I can tell you with any certainty is that they will either stay as they are, or they will disappear completely or they will shrink a little.'

'Ah.' He was clearly disappointed. 'Is there anything I can do to stop them disappearing or shrinking?'

'Wear a good bra, preferably something underwired, to give them plenty of support. That might help preserve the breast tissue – and it will certainly help stop your new breasts from sagging.'

'Oh, I can do that,' said Donyard, a little cheerier now that he was talking about preserving his new breasts. 'I have some very good bras. I've got more bras than Cynthia-Anne. I am to the bra industry what Imelda Marcos is to the shoe industry. Do you realise that without crossdressers the bra industry would collapse? We keep the lingerie makers in business.'

He explained that, according to figures he had read, the average woman thinks she is being rash if she buys one new bra every six months but the average transvestite buys a new bra every two weeks. 'And since one in ten men is a crossdresser, this means that there are almost certainly more men buying bras than there are women buying bras!' said Donyard triumphantly.

'Wear a pink one with a frilly edge,' I said, still trying to get my head round Donyard's astonishing claim.

'Really? Will that make a difference?'

'And make sure it has a little bow at the front – where the two cups meet.'

'Are you serious?'

I looked at him.

'Sorry.' He laughed. 'You were teasing me, weren't you?'

'I was.'

'Any bra will do I guess.'

'I would think so.'

I told him to try not to worry about them disappearing but to enjoy his new breasts for as long as they were there. 'You've risked your life to get them so you might as well take advantage of them.'

'Do you mean that? That I risked my life taking those drugs?'

I nodded.

He paled and said he would make sure that he enjoyed them.

And I did not doubt him for an instant for he was, as I have said, like a boy with a new toy.

Well, to be accurate, he was like a boy with two new toys.

Mr Gibbons

Mr Ezekial Gibbons came in, greeted me and sat down with a sigh.

A general practice surgery is like a lucky dip at a Christmas bazaar in that you never know what you're going to get next. I had been in general practice for some years but I always found a surgery exciting.

Although Mr Gibbons had his 80th birthday a couple of years ago (there was quite a knees-up in the Duck and Puddle to celebrate the occasion) he was very well preserved and really didn't look much over 65.

A keen, amateur historian, he had for nearly 20 years been writing a book on the history of the Corn Laws. The last time we spoke about it he told me that he had written three and a half million words and thought he still had a good deal of work to do before the book would be ready to offer to a publisher. The longest book I'd ever written had been no more than a quarter of a million words and I couldn't imagine how anyone was ever going to understand or edit a book that was over three and a half million words long. If published in full it would, I thought, need to be printed in at least twelve volumes. It seemed a lot of research and writing for one subject.

Mr Gibbons always felt the cold and even when the weather was warm he wore quite a few layers of clothing and it was, for example, quite customary for him to wear two jumpers or waistcoats underneath his suit jacket. He always wore a suit, an old-fashioned hard collar, and a club tie. I had never seen him in casual clothing.

A relatively new resident in Bilbury, Mr Gibbons previously worked as a stockbroker in the City of London and lived in Surrey where he and his wife had a rather large and splendid house – a home big enough to have a billiard room, a library and three staircases. He and his wife were, I believe, members of what was usually referred to as 'The County Set' and their dinner parties had always been reported in society magazines such as *The Tatler*. In the summer, the gardens and grounds of their home were opened to the public. They had several live-in servants, a garage of five luxury cars and a full-time chauffeur.

When his wife died, Mr Gibbons decided he could no longer bear to live in the house they had bought together, decorated together and shared and enjoyed so much and so he took the unusual step of selling it complete with all the contents. Many people sell a house with the carpets and curtains but Mr Gibbons sold his house complete with all the pictures, the furniture, the books, the linen, the crockery and the ornaments. He even left behind most of his clothes and personal items such as old photograph albums.

He once told me that when he left the house he did so carrying an overnight bag containing only a change of clothing, a portable leather chess set which he had carried around with him since boyhood, an old compass which his grandfather had given him, an incunabula which he cherished and a copy of John Bunyan's *Pilgrim Progress*.

He drove to North Devon where his parents had frequently taken him for caravan holidays when he'd been a boy. It was an area of which he had fond and simple memories: days on the beach, surfing on a clumsy wooden board, building sand castles, eating ice cream, fish and chips wrapped in paper.

Memories of places we have visited years before are often a disappointment, of course. Sometimes the place will have changed. Buildings will have been demolished and new ones erected. Roads will have been widened. And sometimes our memories mislead us. We remember things through the eyes of the person we used to be. Our childhood memories in particular are likely to be distorted by time and by affection. We remember only the sunny days. We forget the thunderstorms and the cold winds. We remember the sunshine but we forget the sunburn. We remember the sand dunes but we forget the flies and sharp, spiky grass. We remember the soft sand and we forget the sharp pebbles.

But Mr Gibbons was not betrayed by his memory.

Everything was just as he remembered it. The countryside and the small towns along the North Devon coast had hardly changed in more than half a century. In the small resorts of Ilfracombe, Combe Martin and Lynmouth, a good many of the small pubs and shops which he remembered from his boyhood were still in business. He found a shop where his father had bought him a bucket and a spade.

The shop seemed exactly the same as it had been so many years earlier. The man behind the counter could not possibly have been the same man who had served the very young Ezekial Gibbons but he looked exactly the same. Mr Gibbons told me he thought he may have been the son of the man who had sold him that original bucket and spade. There was an ice cream van parked on the cliffs in exactly the same spot where there had been an ice cream van half a century earlier. It is a fact that over the years, few parts of England have changed as slowly as North Devon.

And then, one dark November evening, Mr Gibbons rediscovered Bilbury.

He found the cottage which his parents had rented when they had a little more money and could upgrade from the caravan they'd usually hired for their annual week by the seaside. And to his astonishment the cottage was still for rent. There had been a faded card stuck to the glass inside the porch and on the card had been a local phone number for prospective tenants to ring. Mr Gibbons rang the number and contacted the owners, who lived in Suffolk, but instead of renting the cottage, he bought it.

Lavender Cottage was an old timber building which was made up of massive beams, measuring around six inches by four inches. Those very old cottages, built on a wooden framework, were all put together in much the same way though heaven knows how the builders moved those massive, enormously heavy beams. I suppose they must have used hand operated winches of some kind. Grooves were cut in the sides of the timbers and hazel rods were fixed into them and then thinner hazel rods were woven in and out, as though a hurdle were being made. The resulting panel was filled with clay or plaster and covered with plaster mixed with animal hair to give it strength.

The cottage had latticed windows, and where a brickwork porch had been added on at some early stage the work had been supported with buttresses. The three granite steps up to the front door were well worn in the middle. An old climbing rose had clambered up the ivy growing on the front and sides of the cottage and, like many ancient rose bushes, it still produced a mass of exquisite flowers in the summertime.

In the reverse of the way that he had sold his old home complete with the contents, so Mr Gibbons bought his cottage complete with all the furniture and other contents. Since the cottage had always been rented to holidaymakers none of the furniture was valuable or even in particularly good condition. Mr Gibbons was convinced that much of the stuff in the cottage was the furniture that he remembered from all those years ago. There was a battered, scarred table in the kitchen and an old Welsh dresser that looked to be almost as old as the cottage. The leather chairs in the sitting room were losing their horse hair stuffing and looked awful but they were still enormously comfortable, and the rug in front of the fireplace was one of those hand-made affairs created out of hundreds of bits of spare material. The iron bedstead in the main bedroom was huge and solid and although the mattress had been renewed many times, there was little doubt that the bedstead had been in situ since Victorian days. In old cottages, with tight winding staircases, the bedframe tends to stay in place for a long time.

'I think my time is nearly up,' said Mr Gibbons. 'I've got one foot in the grave and the other on a banana skin.' He seemed as weary as he sounded and every word seemed to be an effort. 'It's a bugger, isn't it?' He had to stop to take a breath after each sentence. 'As we get old we learn something about the world, we acquire a little knowledge and, hopefully, a touch of wisdom, and then, just as we feel that we are ready to take on the world we find ourselves about to check out. I never really rated him as a critic, I thought him too savage, but old Ruskin was right you know!'

All this was spoken with great effort, as though simply finding the breath was a struggle.

'What did Ruskin say?'

'He said: 'How disgusting it is to find that just when one's getting interested in life one has got to go!''

'You don't look to me as if you are about to go anywhere!' I told him.

And despite the problem he was having with his breathing he didn't look ill. He looked a good colour and he seemed healthy enough. The only change I had noticed was this problem he was clearly having with getting his breath.

'Of course it's different with women,' he said, struggling still. 'Women mature much younger than men, and they're blessed with much more common sense and a greater ability to acquire wisdom at a young age.'

'Mention that to Patsy and Miss Johnson as you leave!' I suggested. 'They'll be fans of yours for eternity.'

'The funny thing is that these days, people are electing younger and younger politicians and company bosses,' said Mr Gibbons. 'And yet it's a strange and unobservant man who knows no more at 70 than he knew at 30!'

'Have you got your list?' I asked him.

Many of my patients came into the surgery with a list of symptoms, signs, worries and medication they needed. Mr Gibbons was one of these. Some doctors objected to patients bringing in a list of symptoms or worries but I never understood why. On the contrary, I rather welcome it and, like Dr Brownlow, I always encouraged patients to write down everything they wanted to tell me and, during the conversation, to write down everything I told them. In fact, I always left a notepad and a pencil on the patient's side of my desk so that they could jot down advice or instructions. It's far too easy to leave the doctor's surgery and subsequently to have to struggle to remember whether the tablets are to be taken before meals, after meals or with meals.

Mr Gibbons, whose memory was still first class, took a small slip of paper out of his inside jacket pocket and handed it to me across the desk. There wasn't much on the paper.

Pain in knee is improving with the aspirin
Varicose veins better now that I'm wearing the elastic stockings
Hearing better after the wax removal

'Splendid!' I said, when I'd read the list. I handed the paper back to him.

He screwed it into a ball and tossed it into my waste paper basket.

'You seem a bit breathless,' I said.

'That's why I think I should be preparing myself for the voyage across the Styx,' he said. 'I'll never finish my book on the damned Corn Laws. I need another six months at least.'

'You didn't put breathlessness on your list?'

'I didn't think there would be anything you could do about it,' he said rather glumly.

I asked him to take off his coat and waistcoats and to let me listen to his chest.

This was not an easy procedure and involved several stoppages while Mr Gibson got his breath. It occurred to me that either both the

81

waistcoats he was wearing had been made for a slimmer man or that maybe Mr Gibbons was no longer the owner of the svelte like figure of which he had once been proud. Simply undoing the buttons took a good deal of effort.

'Two waistcoats?' I said.

'I feel the cold these days,' he explained.

'You could wear a vest or a jumper,' I suggested. 'It would save you a good deal of buttoning and unbuttoning.'

Mr Gibbons agreed that this seemed a moderately good idea. He then wriggled out of his shirt. This came off a lot easier than the waistcoats.

When he had finally managed to undress, I listened to his heart and his lungs.

To my surprise, everything seemed fine. His heart was ticking when it should have been ticking, and tocking when it needed to tock.

And, as I had rather suspected it might be, his breathing was considerably easier than it had been a few minutes earlier.

'Put on your things,' I told him.

Mr Gibbons got dressed. This took quite a while. The shirt wasn't too difficult but the waistcoats were tricky. They were both so tight that Mr Gibbons had great difficulty in buttoning them up. When he'd finished, he was exhausted and sat for a while before putting on his jacket.

'Are those new?' I asked him, suddenly realising that there was another possible explanation for the fact that the waistcoats were so tight.

'I bought them recently,' he told me, looking down, clearly rather pleased with them. 'They're a bit snug and the shop assistant agreed they were probably a size too small but he insisted that the well-fitted look is fashionable this year.'

Once he was dressed, Mr Gibbons started to strain for breath.

'Have you not noticed that your breathing gets more difficult when you are wearing those two waistcoats?'

He nodded. 'I hadn't. But, do you know, you're right!'

He was having so much difficulty in breathing that it was clearly quite a trial for him to say anything.

'If you were to leave off the waistcoats then you would feel a lot healthier,' I told him. 'The waistcoats are so tight they are squeezing your chest and making it difficult for you to breathe properly.'

Mr Gibbons, clearly surprised, looked at me.

'Really!' I said. 'I'll prove it to you.'

I took a simple and rather primitive peak flow meter off my desk and asked Mr Gibbons to breathe into and out of the device. I then wrote down the measurements.

'Now undo those darned waistcoats!'

With a rather weary sigh, Mr Gibbons unbuttoned the two waistcoats.

I then got him to breathe into the peak flow meter and took a fresh set of measurements.

And once that was done I showed him the results. Without the waistcoats the readings were much, much better. Actually, I didn't really need the peak flow meter. Mr Gibbons was breathing much more easily now that the waistcoats were unbuttoned.

'Those waistcoats are too tight for you!' I explained. 'They're preventing your chest from expanding properly. If you leave them off, or at least unbuttoned, then you'll be able to breathe much more easily.'

'I can't believe it!' said Mr Gibbons. He took a really deep breath and smiled with delight. 'You've cured me by removing my waistcoats!' He immediately took them off.

I told him it was the first successful double waistcoatectomy ever performed in South West England and gave him a jumper of mine to wear under his jacket while he went home. In return, he assured me that I could keep the two waistcoats (which were expensive and fancy) for the next Bilbury Hospital Bring and Buy sale.

A Bring and Buy sale is the rich Aunt of the Jumble Sale and, as such, the goods on offer are generally required to be either of superior quality or rather close to new. These two waistcoats fitted into both categories.

It was one of the strangest 'cures' I ever effected.

But, in its own, strange way, it was one of the most pleasing.

The Peripatetic Poet

Thumper Robinson, Patchy Fogg, Frank Parsons, 'Harry' Stottle and I were sitting in the snug of the Duck and Puddle one chilly, late autumn day when a stranger walked in.

We didn't get many strangers in the Duck and Puddle outside the summer season and the newcomer, something of a rarity on a miserable day, was greeted warmly.

'Harry' Stottle, the newly hired barman (who had, in a previous life, been known as Dr Eckersley and had been employed as a Professor of Psychiatry at a London teaching hospital) levered himself out of his chair, walked over to the bar, raised the hatch and stood waiting for the newcomer's instructions.

'What do you recommend?' asked the man, who was a tall, thin fellow with a headful of black, curly hair and a couple of days' growth of a dark beard. He was, I suppose, in his mid-60s and had a nose which looked as though it had been broken at least twice. He was wearing well-worn, bottle-green, corduroy trousers and a very well-worn sports jacket with leather elbow patches. Neither the trousers nor the jacket was a good fit and it seemed a fair guess that both items had been acquired second hand. He had an old, worn rucksack hanging from one shoulder. Judging by its shape, there didn't seem to be a great deal inside it. He had no other luggage with him but when I looked out of the window I saw that outside, in the pub car park, a very old Sunbeam Talbot was parked. Behind the Sunbeam, a huge car of indeterminate colour and blessed with many dents, there was the smallest caravan I'd ever seen in my life. The newcomer was accompanied by a large, weary looking dog.

'If you like beer then you won't be disappointed by a pint of 'Old Restoration', said 'Harry'.

'How much is that?' asked the newcomer, taking a very small handful of coins from his trouser pocket and fingering them carefully.

'Harry' told him the price.

If Frank hadn't been present, 'Harry' would have probably given the stranger the beer without charge. 'Harry' regarded himself more as a host than as a barman and frequently poured drinks for people without asking them to pay. When he had abandoned his life in London, 'Harry' had sold an expensive house and cashed in all his investments. He was, by Bilbury standards, extremely well off. When Frank became aware that 'Harry' was giving beer away (after three whole days had gone by without him finding a single penny in the till he could hardly not notice) he talked to 'Harry' about the basic, commercial principles of running a pub. To Frank's surprise, 'Harry', after promising to do his best to break himself of this bad habit, suggested that he pay £50 a week into the till to cover any occurrences which slipped through. Frank immediately accepted the very generous offer. It did not seem to occur to either of them that 'Harry' was effectively paying for the privilege of working at the Duck and Puddle.

'Just a half then,' said the newcomer.

'Give him a pint on the house,' said Frank.

Patchy, Thumper and I looked at him, astonished. Frank was not normally a plenitudinous man, though it occurred to me a little later that 'Harry's' £50 a week had probably made him more comfortable about such random acts of generosity.

The newcomer, surprised, looked across at the landlord.

'We don't like people drinking halves in here,' said Frank. 'Especially travellers who appear to be a bit down on their luck.'

'Ne'er comes the night ere leaves the day!' said the newcomer, as though this meant something. 'Could I borrow a bowl or a saucer from you?' He nodded towards the dog. 'For my companion.'

'Water?' asked 'Harry' producing a saucer from behind the bar. Frank always kept a couple of bowls there so that he could give water to visiting dogs.

'If you have no objection I will share this excellent looking beverage with my friend,' said the newcomer.

When 'Harry' had handed him the saucer he poured in as much beer as the saucer would take. It is not easy to pour liquid from a beer glass but he somehow managed it without spilling one drop. He then put the saucer down on the floor. The dog looked up, the man nodded his permission, and the dog started lapping at the beer.

'And what's your name, stranger?' asked Frank.

I thought it sounded like a line from a cowboy movie; the sort of line that might have been uttered by John Wayne holding a frontier rifle and stern look. 'What's your name, stranger?'

'My name, the one I carved on my desk at school, is Sid Fish,' came the rather strange reply. 'And my companion is called Bismark.'

Mr Fish's dog, an appropriately shaggy beast, seemed to have had parents of very different origins. One parent had clearly been a German shepherd and the other may have been a collie. 'He's German so when he barks he goes voof voof,' said Mr Fish later.

The dog was deaf, had poor eyesight, and was lazy and friendly with everyone. Later that day, when Bismark was lying in front of the fire in the Duck and Puddle, I saw a ginger cat sleeping on the dog's back – as though he were a large rug. I have no idea where the cat came from or to whom he belonged.

The man and his dog seemed to share everything.

If Mr Fish slept in his caravan (which was, I discovered later, so small that he had to sleep with his feet sticking out of the back window) then Bismark slept in the caravan with him. If Mr Fish slept in a bed then the dog slept on the bed. If Mr Fish slept rough in a barn then the dog slept alongside him on the straw. If Mr Fish had a sausage or a pie then the dog would get a neatly, fairly divided half of what had been served. If someone bought him a beer than Mr Fish would pour a goodly portion of it into a saucer for the dog. The dog had an affection for beer and at one point sat and drank the drips from the tray under the taps in the Duck and Puddle. Mr Fish said that only once had he seen the dog too drunk to walk in a straight line.

Thumper, speaking with affection and no rancour, described the animal as a mongrel and Mr Fish insisted that if the dog were to be described at all it should be called a 'dog of indeterminate, mixed breeding heritage'.

Bismark, we were to discover, may have been lazy but he was doubtless intelligent. If he wanted to go out he would sit and bark but if no one came he was perfectly capable of opening a door himself. He would reach up and hang on the handle until the door opened. Amazingly, I even saw him open a door which was fitted with a knob rather than a handle. Mr Fish said that Bismark could open the door to the Sunbeam Talbot (to get in or to get out) and the door to the small caravan.

After Frank had introduced us all, Mr Fish told us that he originally came from Manchester where his family ran a plumbing business, that he had skilfully side-stepped attempts to persuade him to enter the plumbing trade and that he had worked for a while as an estate agent and a taxi driver.

'I went to London at the age of 28 with a return railway ticket in my pocket. I never used the return half. I have lived by my poetry, my prose and my wits and survived by turning every disappointment into an opportunity. Today,' he said, 'I am a travelling poet and epitaphist. While I am here in Devon, I shall call myself Devonshire's Peripatetic Poet. When I was in Somerset, I was Somerset's Peripatetic Poet. If I go to Cornwall, I shall be the Cornwall's Peripatetic Poet. Devon, of course, is my very most favourite part of the world.'

He smiled and winked as if to say that he knew that we knew that he made these complimentary remarks about every county he visited but that he knew that we would forgive him because of his curiously disarming honesty.

'If I stay here you will find out that I am full to the brim with catarrh, wit and bullshit.' He said this and then laughed loudly and smiled at us all, pleased to share with us his gentle deceits.

We looked and listened. I don't think any of us, not even 'Harry' Stottle, had ever come across anyone quite like him.

'Did you say you wrote epitaphs?' asked Patchy.

'Indeed, I did say that. I am proud to be England's only travelling epitaphist.'

'You write epitaphs for gravestones?'

'Exactly.'

'Is there much of a market for that?'

'Not a big market,' he admitted. 'But more of a market than you would perhaps envisage. Writing inscriptions for graves has always been a well-known occupation for travelling poets.'

'How do you find your customers?' asked Frank.

'I pop into local churches and chapels and have a word with the vicar. I keep my ears open and sometimes if I hear of someone who is very old and frail, I will ask them if they'd like their epitaph writing so that it's ready for the sad moment.'

'That's a bit ghoulish isn't it?' said Patchy.

'Not a bit of it,' said Mr Fish. 'I think of myself as offering an essential public service. It can ease the mind of a dying patient to know that when they have passed on to a better place the bereaved ones they have left behind will not be forced to struggle to find a few suitable words for the gravestone.'

'I always thought I'd just have my name and my dates on mine,' said Thumper. 'It would save a lot of money. Those gravestone people charge an arm and a leg for every letter they chisel on a gravestone.'

'I think it gives a person some comfort to know what will be said about them when they are gone,' said Mr Fish. 'We all worry about how we'll be remembered. It's only natural.'

For a few moments we amused ourselves by thinking up epitaphs for people we knew.

'His parsnips were often a bit woody but they were never cheap,' Thumper offered, as an epitaph for Peter Marshall.

'Here rests Thumper,' suggested Patchy. 'It was the thing he did best.'

'Give us an example of one of your recent epitaphs,' suggested 'Harry'.

'Oh, they are all personalised,' said Mr Fish with apparent, rare modesty. 'I talk to family members and friends and find out a little about my subjects. If they're still alive I talk to the subject themselves and find out how they'd like to be remembered.'

'Give us an example,' insisted 'Harry'.

Mr Fish rummaged in the pocket of his jacket and pulled out an old envelope. 'Here's one I did for a woman in Porlock,' he said, explaining unnecessarily that Porlock is a small village on the North Somerset coast.

The poet and peripatetic epitaphist then read out the epitaph he'd written.

Herein lies old Mother Kent
Time to go so off she went
Made fine cakes and excellent bread
Always did just what she'd said
And paid on time what she'd been lent

When he'd finished, Mr Fish put the piece of paper away in his pocket. 'That's just an example,' he said modestly. 'I must have written hundreds of epitaphs over the years.'

'Very impressive,' said Frank, who is not a literary man and who did seem genuinely impressed.

'She sounds to have been a woman with really good qualities,' said Patchy, who was clearly struggling to keep a straight face.

'Do you ever find that your customers are disappointed with your efforts?' asked 'Harry'.

'Indeed she was. Very, very rarely,' said Mr Fish, answering Patchy and 'Harry' at once and creating a little confusion by so doing. 'But I never give up. Unless, of course, the going gets too tough to be comfortable and then I endeavour to be somewhere else.' He smiled at his remark. There were lots of teeth in the smile. Although they didn't look real, they really were well-made, well-kept teeth. They rather reminded me of Logan Berry's teeth. Actually, I suppose that if you can tell that they're well-made then they can't be, can they?

Mr Fish sighed. 'But, generally speaking, there's no point in letting things get you down, is there?'

Despite the presence of rather too many teeth, it was, I thought, a superficially charming smile and I suspected that wherever he went Mr Fish probably did well with the local ladies. I don't know why but I also suspected even then that it was his charm for the ladies which probably explained his peripatetic way of life.

'And your poems? Do you sell those, too?'

'Oh yes! I have little books of my poems printed and I sell them for half a crown each wherever I go.'

'Recite one of your poems for us!' said Patchy.

'I've already written one for North Devon,' said Mr Fish.

'What's it called?' asked Frank.

'It's called *North Devon*.'

'Good,' said Frank. 'That's a good start. Good title! Say it out loud for us then.'

Mr Fish cleared his throat, as people do when about to start a recitation in public.

'Stark, rock-strewn coves
Wind-swept, sunburnt moors
Hedges high as a tall man's head

In a storm tossed land ruled by nature's laws
Granite cliffs and majestic skies
Seas that pound on empty shores
Narrow paths fit only for goats and sheep
Ferns and bracken decorating bold, stark tors.'

It was generally agreed that this was rather good, though Frank said he had been rather expecting more rhyming.

'Oh, I've got rhyming ones,' said Mr Fish. And he proceeded to recite three more of what he called poems but which I suspect most people would describe as limericks.

'This one is called *A New Bloke* said the poet.

'A randy young woman from Wales
Bought a new bloke in the sales
He had only one eye
But was quite a nice guy
And the best of available males'

'And this one is called *Tears*.'

'A girl with no teeth and small ears
Had a lot of suppressed inner fears
She worried a lot
Whether worth it or not
And often she burst into tears'.

'I say,' said Thumper, who likes limericks, though usually prefers them to be about vicars' daughters and to conclude with a rude punch line, 'that's rather good!'

Encouraged, Mr Fish recited another of his poems. He told us that this one was called *The Burglar*.

'There was a young burglar called Lynn
Who was most unusually thin
She could slide under doors
And slip down through floors
So the police locked her up in a tin

At the conclusion of this short recitation, Mr Fish opened his rucksack and took out a small bundle of booklets. Each booklet bore the title *The People's Poet*, with Sid Fish below it in large letters and the price (2 shillings and 6 pence) clearly printed in the bottom right hand corner. Mr Fish then handed one to each of us.

He called them books but they were no more than 16 pages in length which made them a little on the skimpy side for books and rather generous for leaflets.

'These are first editions and will be valuable if I ever become Poet Laureate,' he assured us.

'You haven't gone decimal then?' said Frank. He pointed to the price marked on the cover.

'Oh no! I prefer to stick to old-fashioned money,' said Mr Fish. 'My customers are mostly older folk and they're accustomed to thinking in terms of half crowns, ten bob notes and so on.'

'I haven't got half a crown,' said Patchy, pulling some coins out of his pocket. 'Will 50 pence do?'

'That will be fine,' said Mr Fish, taking the coin and slipping it into his jacket pocket with the ease of a magician performing a parlour trick.

To be honest, I don't think any of us really wanted his books of poems but we all bought one and we all paid 50 pence which had, thanks to Patchy, become the going price. I suspected that Mr Fish, now richer by a modest but doubtless tax-free £2, had been clever in pricing his booklets at 'half a crown'. Since no one would actually have half a crown to give him, and since 20 pence looked far too mean (even though it was actually the equivalent of more than half a crown) most people would pay him 50 pence or even a pound. It is, of course, possible that the books had been printed before the introduction of the decimal currency for they bore no date.

'Splendid stuff!' said 'Harry', who had opened his book and was reading the first poem.

'Some of my poetry is autobiographical,' said Mr Fish. He told us that he had lived a life of quiet but unending disappointments, frustrations, failures, rejections and broken promises but that he always tried to remain cheerful.

'I'll read mine later,' said Thumper, slipping his booklet into his pocket. He sounded very convincing but the idea of Thumper ever reading a book of poetry, however slender the book might be, made me want to laugh.

'A chap in Wales told me that any fool could have written these,' said Mr Fish. 'And I told him that though what he said was probably true he had to agree that it would take a clever man to sell them to other fools.'

And then the smile was there again.

'I can see that you are all gentlemen of learning, intellectuals of discernment,' he said. 'And I am sure that you could all write better verse but could you sell it?'

'Almost certainly not!' I agreed, looking through Mr Fish's small book. The poems were a mixture of limericks and doggerel with a few one-liners and epitaphs thrown in for good measure. We all read quietly for a few moments, then put our booklets away. We all offered polite congratulations.

'Harry' Stottle, the barman and exiled psychiatrist, later said that Mr Fish rather reminded him of Mark Tapley, the wonderful character in Dickens's *Martin Chuzzlewit* who regarded every setback and disappointment as a challenge, and who took great pride in his ability to hold his head up high when things went badly.

I remembered Mark Tapley, with great affection for he is one of my favourite fictional inventions.

'There's no credit in being jolly' protests Mr Tapley, when he is staying in a comfortable inn. 'There might be some credit in being jolly with a wife, especially if the children have the measles and that and was very fractious indeed'.

Even when he is desperately ill, Tapley remains remorselessly upbeat and incorrigibly upbeat. Asked how he is, Tapley, on his sick bed, replies: 'Floored for the present, sir, but jolly!'

'Where are you heading after Bilbury?' asked Patchy

'Oh, I'm on a mystery tour,' said Mr Fish. 'And it's as much a mystery to me as it is to yourselves.' He paused, sipped a little of his beer and sighed contentedly. I got the feeling that he would have liked to drain the glass but that he wanted to savour the beer and wasn't sure that he would be offered another. 'People search constantly for something without ever knowing what it is they are looking for and I am no exception. But maybe I have already found that which I seek but have not yet realised the extent of my discovery. Did you know that, according to legend, the musk deer wanders the forests constantly searching for the source of the beautiful odour it can smell, but never realises that the scent is its own?'

He had a beautiful speaking voice and the voice managed to give some semblance of good sense and meaning to the bits of pieces of cod-philosophy he produced. It was the voice of an actor or broadcaster. He had picked up bits and pieces of accents from his travels and you would never guess that he originally hailed from Lancashire. There were tastes of Gloucestershire, hints of Ireland and occasionally a word or a phrase would remind me of the Midlands, London or Wales.

'Do you enjoy writing poetry?' asked Frank.

'Oh, I do,' said Mr Fish. 'Don't you remember sweet Alice, Ben Holt, Sweet Alice whose hair was so brown, who wept with delight when you gave her a smile, and trembled with fear at your frown.'

'That sounds like Thomas Dunn English,' said 'Harry' immediately.

Mr Fish, clearly startled, looked at him.

'The American politician and poet,' explained 'Harry'.

'Indeed it is, sir, it is a poem from that much loved man and I congratulate you on your knowledge and your memory! I carry so much poetry in my head that I sometimes forget which is mine and which is another's. But, of course, I simply quoted that particular poem to give you the flavour of a style which I myself aim to emulate. My poetry is my madness.'

He had, I thought, escaped reasonably well from the mild charge of attempted plagiarism.

'I understand,' nodded 'Harry', magnanimously. 'Perhaps no person can be a poet, or even enjoy poetry, without a certain unsoundness of mind.'

Mr Fish looked at him. 'I beg your pardon?'

'Macaulay,' explained 'Harry'.

'Oh, of course,' said Mr Fish. 'I'm not too hot on American writers.'

'Not exactly American,' said 'Harry'. 'He was an English poet, essayist historian and politician. He lived in the 19th century and perhaps better known as Baron Macaulay.'

'Oh, that Macaulay!' said Mr Fish. 'Oh, yes of course. He's one of my favourites.'

He tried to make it look convincing but he overdid it and we all knew he'd never heard of Lord Macaulay.

We all sat in the Duck and Puddle for another hour or so and I bought a round of drinks. Then Mr Fish said that he'd better see about finding somewhere to park his caravan and Frank said that he could leave it where it was if he was only staying for a day or two.

All that happened on the Saturday.

I next saw Mr Fish on the following Tuesday when I was driving into Barnstaple to visit the dentist for my annual check-up.

I was just heading out of the village when I spotted Mr Fish standing by the side of the road. He had his thumb out, in the class hitchhiker pose, and his dog by his side. I confess that I almost didn't stop. I knew that he had been going door to door around the village, selling his poems and trying to sell his unwritten epitaphs. Some of the people to whom he'd sold poems really couldn't afford to buy them – and certainly didn't want them – but I had heard one or two tales of him using sales techniques which even Peter Marshall would have found questionable. He told two people that he was in the village at the invitation of Frank and me and that he was selling his poems for charity. I don't believe he ever gave a penny to any charity other than himself. Worse still, I heard that he had harassed a couple of people whose relatives had died recently. He had, I think, got their names from the church burial register. He certainly didn't get the names from me. He hadn't sold either of them one of his epitaphs – mainly because everyone in the village knows that every letter and number carved on a headstone costs money. 'Harry' told me, in confidence, that he didn't like Mr Fish one little bit, that he no longer reminded him of Mark Tapley and that he thought the bonhomie was entirely fake. 'He is a chancer,' said 'Harry'. 'I wouldn't trust him as far as I could throw him.'

But I knew that there was no bus to Barnstaple that day and I felt sorry for Mr Fish and so I stopped.

As man and dog climbed into my 1930 Rolls Royce 20/25, with Mr Fish sitting in the passenger seat and his dog curled up at his feet, the poet explained that his car was rather short of petrol and he was a little low on funds.

'Where are you headed?' I asked.

'I'm going into Barnstaple.'

'No problem. I can take you and drop you wherever you like.'

He looked around, searching for something. 'Where's the seat belt?'

'I'm afraid there isn't one. Cars this age don't have to have them fitted.'

He didn't seem bothered by this and just sat back. 'This is a lovely old car!'

I explained that the car had been bequeathed to me by my predecessor, Dr Brownlow and that although it was too large for the lanes and very heavy on petrol I kept it largely for sentimental reasons.

'I'm going to see an old flame,' he told me, as we motored along. 'Well, she was more than an old flame. She was my first love and we were going to get married.'

'She's local?'

'Oh yes. She's a Devon girl through and through.'

'I didn't know you'd been down in this part of Devon before.'

'It was quite a few years ago. And there aren't many parts of England I've not visited. I don't know why so many people take all their holidays abroad. There are so many wonderful places to see in England. If I want to go abroad I go to Wales or Scotland!'

I agreed with him.

'Her mother refused to let us marry,' said Mr Fish. 'She said that her daughter was too young and that I was too unreliable.' He paused, deep in thought. 'Charlotte was 18 so I don't think she was too young.'

'Charlotte was your girlfriend?'

'Yes. Lovely name isn't it?'

'She won't be too young now!' I pointed out.

'No, she won't!' Mr Fish laughed. 'And her mother died a few years ago so that won't be a problem. Believe me, I wouldn't be going there if her mother was still alive! She was a huge woman, quite short but weighing in at least twenty stone. She was an old battle-axe; a wild woman, forever screaming and shouting and threatening to do terrible things to everyone around her. I never saw her without her hair in curlers and food stains down the front of her pinafore.' He stopped, remembering times past. 'I never understood how such a hideous harridan could have possibly mothered such a sweet and gentle girl.'

'How do you know Charlotte isn't married?'

'I spoke to a chap I know who lives nearby and managed to find her phone number. I rang her up last week.'

'So she knows you're coming to see her?'

'Oh yes. I said it would be sometime in the afternoon but I'm sure she won't mind if I get there an hour or two early.'

'And she's not married?'

'She's divorced with one kid – a daughter. The husband was a wastrel who buggered off years ago. They were only married for eighteen months or so. He went off with a woman from the local chip shop.'

I didn't say anything but I couldn't help thinking that for Mr Fish to describe another man as a wastrel might be construed by some as fitting into the category of 'the pot calling the kettle black'.

'And how long is it since you saw her?' I asked.

Mr Fish thought for a while. 'It must be nearly twenty years.'

As I drove along the lanes, Mr Fish told me a little more about the woman he was going to see. Charlotte was, he said, a pretty, slim girl with blonde, shoulder length hair and blue eyes; gentle and quiet and always laughing and full of fun. 'She would never hurt a flea,' he said. 'I very much liked that about her. She found a mouse in the kitchen once. She was terrified of it but she managed to catch it in a cardboard box and put it outside in the garden. She was so gentle with it.'

I couldn't help wondering how Mr Fish had known about the business with the mouse. I rather suspected that he had probably been standing a yard or two away, watching from a safe distance.

When I eventually managed to park the car in Barnstaple (never easy since the car is so huge and the spaces so small that I have to try to find two spaces and then buy two tickets – ideally I need four spaces but that never happens) a by now excited Mr Fish got out and asked me if I knew where he could find Barbican Road where Charlotte lived. We were so close I could point to where he could find it.

'Do you want a lift back or will you be staying in Barnstaple?' I asked him. 'I shouldn't be more than an hour. After I've been to the dentist I just need to pop into a stationery store to pick up some bits and pieces I need for the surgery but I'll be heading back to Barnstaple in about sixty minutes or so.'

'If I'm coming back to Bilbury I'll be here by your car in an hour,' replied Mr Fish. 'If I'm not here then you can assume I'm staying and I'll be back in Bilbury tomorrow to fetch my car and caravan.'

And so off I went to the dentist.

To my delight, all was well. No extractions and no fillings. There are few simple joys to exceed the joy of walking out of a dental surgery with a clean bill of tooth. I immediately wandered across the road to a small, conveniently situated sweet shop and bought a quarter of a pound of old-fashioned humbugs, sold loose in a small, white paper bag. The woman behind the counter, who looked as though she had sampled everything on her shelves and whose figure had paid the price, told me that having a dentist's surgery across the road was wonderful for business. She said that patients either came to her shop to celebrate or to cheer themselves up after being told that they needed to have treatment. I told her that she should pay the dentist a commission and she said that he too was a regular customer and that she always gave him a discount.

I then wandered into the town, sucking on a tooth rotting humbug but not giving a damn because my teeth had just been given a clean bill of health, and bought a new typewriter ribbon, a large packet of envelopes and half a dozen cheap ball point pens for Miss Johnson to use. I don't know where they all go but we seem to get through more cheap ballpoint pens than makes any sort of sense. If I saw drug company representatives I would doubtless be provided with an endless supply of ballpoint pens decorated with advertising slogans. But I don't see any drug company salesmen and I happily buy my own pens.

When I got back to the Rolls Royce, Mr Fish was sitting on the passenger side running board waiting for me. He looked as if he had been there some time.

'You're coming back to Bilbury?' I said, rather unnecessarily.

He just nodded.

I opened the car and we both got in. I took the packet of humbugs out of my pocket and offered him one. He shook his head but said nothing. He looked like a man in shock; as though he had seen a ghost. There was no point in asking him how things had gone since they had obviously not gone to plan.

'I had a bit of a surprise,' he said, ten minutes into our journey.

I didn't say anything but just waited for him to continue.

'I knocked on the door and I had the shock of my life,' he said. 'It was opened by Charlotte. I couldn't believe my eyes.'

I looked across at him. He seemed dazed.

97

'She hadn't changed. She was exactly the same: slim, beautiful, blonde hair, blue eyes and a wonderful figure.'

There was a long silence. He was obviously still coming to terms with what had happened.

'She looked eighteen. She hadn't changed a bit. Not a bit. She was still the same. Nothing had altered. I nearly fainted when I saw her. It did not seem possible.'

Mr Fish's story was now fascinating me. Was there a picture in the attic? Was this a female version of Oscar Wilde's 'Dorian Gray'? Had Charlotte undergone plastic surgery? Or was the truth, perhaps, that Mr Fish had 'seen' not what he really saw but what he'd expected or hoped to see?

'When she opened the door the girl was smiling,' continued Mr Fish. 'She was clearly expecting someone and for a brief moment I thought it was me that she was hoping to see. But, sadly, I quickly realised that I wasn't the person for whom she was smiling. Within a second the smile had faded, there was disappointment in her eyes and a frown had appeared. She asked who I was and what I wanted but before I could reply there was a scream from the back part of the house, from the kitchen probably.'

'A scream?'

'Well not so much a scream, I suppose. It was more of a screech. It was a woman shouting abuse. The only bit I managed to hear was: 'If that's your bastard fancy man you can tell him to bugger off!''

I swerved around a cyclist who was wobbling all over the road as though he'd had a little too much to drink.

'I looked at the girl standing in the doorway,' continued Mr Fish. 'And suddenly she looked tired and downtrodden. The joy had completely gone from her eyes. 'That's my mother,' she explained. 'She thinks you're my boyfriend.'

Mr Fish said the girl told him that her mother didn't approve of her boyfriend, that he was in a band and that he was a bit older than she was. He told me that the girl said that the two of them wanted to get married but that her mother disapproved of her even seeing the man.

'I asked her why she didn't just leave home and go off with her bloke,' said Mr Fish. 'Do you know what she said?'

Naturally, I said I didn't.

'She said she didn't know why but she just couldn't. It was exactly what Charlotte said to me 20 years ago. She didn't know why but she just couldn't.'

Belatedly, I was now beginning to realise what had happened. Charlotte didn't have a picture hanging in the attic. And she hadn't had cosmetic surgery.

'The girl's mother was your Charlotte?'

'Yes.'

His voice was so quiet I could hardly hear what he said.

'Did you see Charlotte?'

'I caught a glimpse of her for a brief moment. She suddenly appeared in the hallway behind her daughter.'

'Her hair was in curlers?'

'Oh, yes. Her hair was in curlers and I'd swear she had egg down the front of her jumper. She'd doubled in size and she had a face just like her mother's: full of hatred.'

I didn't say anything.

'The hatred and loathing and disappointment were all that were left. The girl was the spitting image of her mother and Charlotte had become her own mother – even down to interfering with her own daughter's relationship.'

'Did you speak to Charlotte?'

'No, no! I muttered something about having called at the wrong house. I said I was looking for a man called George who had an old Ford Popular for sale.'

'And you left?'

'I scurried down the path and went straight to your car. I was back in the car park within ten minutes of leaving it.'

'I'm sorry,' I said.

There was silence for another couple of miles.

'Never mind,' said Mr Fish at last. 'It wouldn't have worked out anyway. I've been footloose for too long. A girl in every port, that's me.'

I turned and saw him grinning at me. 'Did you say you had some humbugs?'

I took the white bag out of my pocket and handed it to him.

When we got back to Bilbury, I dropped Mr Fish off at the Duck and Puddle where his car and caravan were still parked. He was jolly and seemed cheerful but I could tell he was rather miserable and desperately disappointed. He had, I suppose, been hoping he could recapture and revitalise some lost memories. And because I felt sorry for him I gave him a few pounds to buy petrol.

That was on the Tuesday.

On the Saturday of that week, the sixth day of Mr Fish's stay in Bilbury, I discovered why he never stayed long in one place and why his nose looked such a mess.

Patsy, Anne (Thumper's wife), Thumper and I were all standing at the bar in the Duck and Puddle. Patsy and Anne had called at the pub on their way into Barnstaple, where they both intended to buy hats for a wedding, and they had called into the pub to let Thumper and me know where they were going. Patsy had a small glass of white wine and Anne was drinking half a pint of shandy (which contained considerably more lemonade than beer). Patsy was wearing a wonderful frock made by a fairly new company called Laura Ashley. Anne who is notably zaftig was wearing a very tight jumper and a very tight skirt.

Suddenly, Mr Fish appeared as though from nowhere, wandered up to the bar and stood beside Anne. Since I knew he wouldn't have any money or not want to spend whatever he had, I told 'Harry' the barman to give him whatever he was drinking. He had already shown that he had an uncanny knack of turning up when he thought there might be a free drink available.

But even before 'Harry' could finish pouring the pint of Old Restoration which Mr Fish had requested, Anne jumped and yelped. Without pausing, without any hesitation at all, she backed away from the bar and slapped Mr Fish on the cheek.

It was all very impressive and she had moved with astonishing speed. It was a hell of a slap, too.

'He pinched my bum!' she cried, explaining to the rest of us why she had reacted so sharply and dramatically. 'The cheeky old bugger pinched my bum!'

'I'm sorry!' said Mr Fish, rubbing his cheek rather ruefully. 'Force of habit. I didn't think you'd mind.'

Frozen in disbelief we all looked at him.

'Come over here,' said Thumper quietly. He didn't raise his voice and he didn't look or sound particularly angry. He pointed to an area in the pub where there was more room. He thought for a moment and then moved a table and a couple of chairs so that there was even more space available.

Mr Fish looked at Thumper, who was the best part of a foot taller than him, considerably heavier and far more menacing. 'I'm so sorry,' he said, apologising again. 'I think maybe it's time I moved on.'

'It is time you moved on but before you go I'm going to punch you,' said Thumper. 'You can fight or you can defend yourself or you can just stand there. But I'm going to punch you.'

'I am so sorry,' said Mr Fish, apologising yet again. 'I didn't mean to cause offence.'

'I'm not sure that I like you,' said Thumper. 'I think you're probably a liar and a bit of a crook but you're not a young man. You're smaller than I am and you're not in good shape. Superficially, you're an amiable, likeable, cheeky sort of fellow and in a strange sort of way it will be a pleasure to see you when you come back to this part of the world. Nevertheless, I'm going to punch you and then you're going to leave Bilbury and head for Cornwall or wherever else you fancy. And if and when you come back you'll remember the lesson and you'll behave yourself a little more like a gentleman.'

This was one of the longest speeches I'd ever heard from Thumper.

'But your wife has already slapped me!' protested Mr Fish. 'It was a good slap, too!'

He was right about it being a good slap. The red palm print was still visible. I got the impression it wasn't the first time he'd been slapped.

'I don't want to do this,' said Thumper, who looked as if he genuinely didn't want to hit Mr Fish. 'But I have no choice. I have to punch you or you might tell people you disrespected me and I did nothing about it. More importantly, I will feel deeply offended for a long time and that won't be good for me.'

'I've apologised,' said Mr Fish.

'Come over here,' said Thumper, pointing to the empty area of the pub again. 'I don't want you banging your head on the bar when you go backwards.'

'Why am I going to bang my head on the bar?' asked Mr Fish, rather weakly.

'My wife gave you a good slap because you offended her and she can and does look after herself,' pointed out Thumper. 'But she's my wife and so this is for offending me.'

And since Mr Fish showed absolutely no sign of wanting to fight, or even any inclination to defend himself, Thumper then hit the poet and epitaph writer plumb on the nose. He hit him with a rather gentle right hook which was delivered with such quiet, controlled efficiency that everyone who saw it winced. Thumper's elbow went no further back than the side of his chest and he put very little effort into the punch. Mr Fish's dog, Bismark, watched the whole episode and clearly had no intention of interfering.

I now knew precisely how and why Thumper had acquired his nickname.

Mr Fish fell backwards and landed, spread-eagled, on Frank and Gilly's rug.

Instinctively, I strode across to where he lay but by the time I'd knelt down to see if he was still alive, he had already raised himself up off the floor. He sat up and gently took hold of his nose between the forefinger and thumb of his right hand. There was surprisingly little blood.

'Is it broken?' he demanded. 'It's broken again isn't it?'

'No, it's not broken,' I told him, a couple of moments later. I was glad about that. I didn't want to have to call an ambulance, and send him to the hospital so that he could have his nose X-rayed.

'Oh good,' said Mr Fish. 'That's OK then.' He wiggled his jaw and massaged his nose. It clearly wasn't the first time he'd been punched on the nose. And on the previous occasions the nose had obviously been broken. He touched his nose again and winced. 'I'll have a good bruise. It'll make me look like an old prize fighter.'

He looked at Thumper, then looked at Anne and then looked at the rest of us.

'I could sue you!' he said to Thumper, quite unexpectedly. 'Assault. I could get damages.'

'What could you sue him for?' I asked.

'For punching me!' said Mr Fish.

'I didn't see anyone punch you,' I told him. I turned to the others. 'Did anyone see Thumper punch Mr Fish?'

'Definitely not,' said 'Harry'.

'No,' said Patchy.

'Absolutely not,' said Patsy and Anne together.

'No one punched you,' said Frank. 'You were a bit tiddly and tripped over your own feet.'

Mr Fish stared at us and then turned on the smile. 'Of course I did,' he said.

At least Mr Fish knew when he was beaten.

He picked up his rucksack and, with Bismark following, he hurried off. He didn't even say 'goodbye'.

For a while, at the beginning, it had been amusing to have him around. But, to be honest, none of us was sad to see him go.

'I only tapped him,' said Thumper.

'Only tapped him!' I said.

'Just a little tap to teach him a lesson,' said Thumper. 'Anne hit him harder than I did.' He finished his pint and held out the empty glass to 'Harry' for a refill.

'Would you have done that, if Mr Fish had pinched my bottom?' Patsy asked me, putting her arm through mine.

'Of course I would!' I replied.

Patsy gave me a squeeze.

We all had another drink and then Patsy and Anne went hat shopping in Barnstaple while Patchy, Thumper, Frank, 'Harry' and I stayed in the cosy snug at the Duck and Puddle and did what we did best: watching logs sizzle and talking about nothing very important.

Crash, Bang, Wallop!

Patsy was the first to wake up.

'Did you hear that?' she whispered?

'Hear what?' I asked, struggling to remember where I was and who I was. I'd been just about to go out and open the batting for England in a Test Match against Australia and I'd been having difficulty in fastening my pads which were, for some strange reason, made of sponge cake. In my dream, having pads made of sponge cake hadn't seemed such a big problem. After all, the ball was made of chocolate and my cricket bat was made of something that looked remarkably like pink marshmallow.

'Behind the wall,' whispered Patsy. 'There's someone on the other side of the wall.'

I woke up suddenly, reached out a hand and switched on my bedside light. Then we lay and listened. Ben, our elderly dog, growled as though he too felt upset by something. He had been sleeping on the bed, next to and sometimes on top of my feet.

After a few moments of lying quietly, listening carefully, I could hear what had woken Patsy but I didn't have the foggiest idea what I was hearing.

'What's behind that wall?' asked Patsy

'Nothing,' I replied. 'It's an outside wall.'

'It sounds as though someone is trying to get through the wall. Do you think it could be a burglar?'

'Why would a burglar try to break through our bedroom wall?'

'I don't know. People do funny things these days.'

'But if it was a burglar wouldn't he try to come in through a downstairs window?' I asked. 'A door would be even easier.'

'Is the front door locked?'

'No, I don't think so. It wasn't windy. And anyway I left the back door wedged slightly open so that the cats can come in and out.'

We only usually locked the front door when the weather was particularly windy, with the wind coming from the south east. This didn't happen too often because our prevailing wind was generally from the south west. We did lock the door when the weather was bad because the catch no longer worked properly and with a south easterly wind the door swung to and fro and banged a good deal. Although I'd tried to mend the catch, my attempts had been notable only for their lack of success. We never locked the back door.

'Why did you leave the back door open? The cats have got a cat flap so that they can come in and out whenever they like!'

'I know. But Jeremy's arthritis is playing up.'

Jeremy is the oldest of our cats. We inherited him from Mrs Arnott-Toynbee who was dying, and who wanted me to put him to sleep so that he could be cremated and buried with her. Her reasons were entirely selfish: she didn't want anyone else to have him. She gave him to me to take home with instructions that I was to put him to sleep and take him back to her in a neat, little, wooden box which she had provided. I'm afraid I cheated. When Mrs Arnott-Toynbee was buried a few days later, she went to her grave clutching the small, wooden box containing ash from our bonfire site. Jeremy was twelve when we acquired him and already had early signs of arthritis in his left leg. Despite our best efforts to treat him, the arthritis has got steadily worse. He can manage the cat flap, in an ungainly sort of way, but if the weather isn't too cold, I leave the back door open for him. Naturally, Emily and Sophie, our other cats, are also happy to avoid the cat flap which I think they find rather undignified and, in truth, a little beneath them.

'I hope we don't get any mice or squirrels wandering in.'

'I don't think we need worry about that,' I assured her. 'Not with three living mouse traps prowling around the kitchen.'

'There! I heard it again,' said Patsy, suddenly sitting up in bed.

I heard it too. It was difficult to describe. There was some scrabbling and some scratching and there was, too, something that sounded as if bits of masonry were falling. The sound definitely reminded me of something but I couldn't remember what.

'Do you think the wall is falling down?' asked Patsy.

'No!' I said, with a definitiveness I did not entirely feel.

'It's a very old house,' Patsy reminded me.

'But it's solid,' I said.

'There's definitely something outside trying to get in through the wall,' insisted Patsy.

And I found it difficult to disagree with her.

'I'd better go outside and have a look,' I said, clambering out of bed and pulling on my clothes. Fortunately, I always kept a pair of trousers, a shirt and a jumper next to the bed so that I could dress quickly in a medical emergency. I looked at the clock. It was a quarter to seven.

I pulled the curtains back an inch, just to see what the weather was like. Dawn had broken and the day was well under way. The weather looked fine: no wind and no rain. I picked up the torch from the bedside table but I put it back realising that I didn't need it.

'Can you see anything?' asked Patsy, after I'd looked out of the window.

'There are no signs that Bilbury has been invaded by fifteen foot tall creatures from outer space,' I assured her. I kissed her and tottered downstairs, closely followed by Ben who was brave enough to come along to help but intelligent enough to realise that hiding behind my legs made better tactical sense than running on ahead.

Outside there was absolutely nothing to see. There were no burglars around. There was no ladder leaning against the side of the house. The flower bed which ran along the side of the house was pristine and untouched. There were no damaged plants and no footprints in the soil. I went back indoors and took a look around. There were no signs that anyone had been into the house. I went back to the bedroom.

'Did you see anything?' asked Patsy.

'Absolutely nothing!'

'I can still hear the noise,' said Patsy, who was now also out of bed and dressed.

I stood and listened for a few moments and then I suddenly realised why the noises seemed familiar.

'It sounds just like that time that Sophie climbed up the chimney, got stuck on a ledge and wouldn't come back down!'

We stood still and listened again.

'You're right,' said Patsy. 'It does sound as if there's something stuck in a chimney.'

'There's only one problem,' I said.

'There's no chimney here!' said Patsy, finishing off the thought for me.

Puzzled, we went downstairs and had an early breakfast.

By the end of the day, when we were still no nearer to thinking of a solution, I telephoned Thumper Robinson to ask if he could think of an explanation.

'Those old houses have massive walls,' he explained. 'Bilbury Grange's walls are nearly three feet thick but when they built houses like yours they usually made the walls with a gap in the middle – just like modern houses. The difference was that a century or two ago, the builders usually filled the gap in the middle with all sorts of leftover rubble. They did this because they believed that filling up the middle of the wall helped keep the cold out and the warmth in. And the walls they built were so thick that they didn't worry much about the damp getting through.'

'Presumably, it also gave them somewhere to dump all their rubble,' I suggested. 'To save them carting the stuff away and then having find somewhere to dump it where they weren't going to get done for fly tipping. I doubt if they called it fly-tipping in the 19th century but they were probably no more enthusiastic about it then than we are now.'

Thumper laughed. 'Exactly!'

'So do you think that's what we heard? Some bits of rubble slipping down the inside of our wall?'

'Probably,' agreed Thumper. 'I'll pop round and have a look. I've got to pass your house because I'm delivering a couple of dozen bales of straw to Tom Gaskin's wife.'

'How is Tom?' I asked.

Tom was a vet who had accidentally injected himself with a lethal dose of pentobarbital intended for his Great Dane. The dog was dying of cancer and Tom had decided to put it to sleep. Unfortunately, Tom was crying so much that he completely missed the dog and injected his own leg with the stuff. I had to climb a hill on their land and put up two saline drips to save his life. His wife had ridden across country to Bilbury Grange to fetch the extra saline that I needed. It had been a dramatic evening.

'He's fine now!' said Thumper. 'Except he was obviously brain damaged by the drug he injected himself with, because he's still suffering from delusions. Actually, they are both deluded because they constantly sing your praises. I told Tom that if he survived your ministrations then it was doubtless more luck than judgement.'

'Thank you,' I said drily.

'Don't mention it,' said Thumper. 'I'll call in on my way back and have a look and then you can give me a glass of something refreshing. I'll need it by the time I've unloaded 24 bales of straw.'

By 'something refreshing', Thumper didn't mean a nice, cool glass of lemonade. And he certainly wasn't referring to 'a nice cup of tea'. What he meant by 'refreshing' was a glass of Old Restoration – then, as now, still his favourite beer. I don't usually drink the stuff but we always keep a crate of it in the larder.

And so later that day, we took Thumper upstairs to listen to the sounds in our bedroom wall. Naturally, by this time the strange sounds had stopped. There was nothing whatsoever to be heard.

'It sounded like a scratching or scrabbling noise,' said Patsy.

'Maybe a mouse or a rat had got into the wall,' said Thumper. 'If they can find a way into the middle of an old wall then they sometimes make a nest there. Nice and dry and sheltered. It could have been a squirrel. Or a bat.'

'Oh dear!' said Patsy. 'You don't think it could be trapped, do you?'

'It won't be trapped,' Thumper assured her. 'But if it was scrabbling about then it might have started a small landslide among the rubble.'

Then we all heard another slight noise. It sounded feebler than before. Thumper heard it too.

'Can I borrow your stethoscope?' Thumper asked me.

Not bothering to ask why, I went downstairs and fetched my stethoscope.

Thumper then put the earpieces into his ears and the business end, the diaphragm, of the stethoscope, against the wall.

'What could you hear?' asked Patsy, when Thumper removed the stethoscope and handed it back to me.

'There's definitely something in there,' he said.

Unexpectedly, he then started tapping the wall. It's a technique all doctors use to see if there is fluid in a chest. You can diagnose the extent of any fluid in the lungs by measuring the change in the sounds. It's a technique that was originally used by beer and wine makers to measure the amount of fluid left in a cask or barrel. Thumper's tapping showed clearly that a piece of the wall about four feet wide and three or four feet high was hollow.

'What is it?' asked Patsy.

And then suddenly she gasped.

'A chimney? Do you think there's a chimney in there?'

'When you bought this place how much work did you do in this room?' asked Thumper.

'We just papered over the existing paper,' I admitted.

'It was dark blue with a gold stripe and looked as if it had been there for about 40 years,' said Patsy. 'We tried to scrape it off but it didn't want to leave.'

'Let's go and have a look outside,' said Thumper.

The three of us trooped downstairs, followed by one dog and two cats, and trotted out into the garden. Thumper then walked around the house counting chimneys. Patsy and I followed him.

'How many fireplaces have you got?' he asked.

'Three,' I replied. 'One in the drawing room, one in the kitchen, one in my consulting room and one in the dining room.'

'That's four,' said Patsy.

'Four,' I agreed.

'You've got sixteen chimney stacks,' said Thumper. 'And since they didn't usually build chimneys without there being a fireplace at the other end there is a fairly good chance that you've got twelve hidden fireplaces.' He looked at me, grinned and leant towards me confidentially. 'That's sixteen minus four,' he said.

I thanked him for the maths lesson.

'So if there is a chimney behind that wall then something could be inside it and trying to get out?' said Patsy.

'Yes,' agreed Thumper. 'The funny thing is that usually when a fireplace has been blocked up there will just be something stuck over the fireplace itself and the chimney breast will still be visible – with an alcove remaining each side. In fact, if a room has an alcove and a chimney breast but no visible fireplace, it's pretty certain that behind the chimney breast there will be a fireplace – quite probably a rather nice, old one. The odd thing with your bedroom is that if there is a fireplace then they covered over the chimney breast and the two alcoves as well – probably with huge pieces of plaster board.'

'So we could have a chimney in our bedroom?'

'Absolutely! And if you took off the plaster board, or whatever is covering up that side of the room then your bedroom would be bigger because you'd regain the two alcoves – one on each side of the chimney breast. Heaven knows what they used to fill the two alcoves.'

'So, how do we find out?' asked Patsy.

'Simple,' said Thumper. 'Where's the biggest hammer you've got?'

Now, at this point it would, of course, have been wise to stop, think and plan our next move. We should, at the very least, have spread some dustsheets over the bed, the carpet and the rest of the furniture in the bedroom. That is doubtless what normal, sensible people would have done. It is certainly what we should have done.

Instead, I hurried downstairs and fetched a sledge hammer from one of the barns.

The sledge hammer I fetched was so huge and so heavy that I hardly ever used it. To be honest, I had a job to raise it up above waist height without toppling backwards and I don't think I ever managed to raise it above shoulder height. I can't even remember how we came by it but I rather suspect it came in with a job lot of elderly garden tools which I purchased at a monthly auction in Lynton; the small holiday resort which is twinned with Lynmouth and which can be found just a few miles eastwards along the coast.

A year or two earlier, I had bought quite a number of our garden tools at two separate auctions – both of them in Lynton. Victorian gardeners had specific tools made for just about everything and some of the tools were very clever and marvellously well designed. So, for example, we have seven different garden forks, seven different types of spade and shovel, five different hoes and four different types of rake. Most people think a spade is a spade is a spade and Gertrude Stein would have doubtless agreed with them, but in our collection we had a digging shovel with a pointed tip (for digging in soft soil), a digging shovel with a square blade (for digging in hard packed soil), a trenching shovel with a sharp tip and square sides, a narrow spade with a rounded tip for transplanting shrubs or planting flowers, a scoop shovel for moving coal, snow or grain, a scraping spade for removing ice or weeds from paths, an edging spade with a half-moon blade and a hinged post hole digging spade. The whole lot cost us no more than a couple of pounds.

Many people who go to auctions are looking for elegant pieces of furniture, impressive paintings or potentially valuable pieces of silver, pottery or jewellery but it is often possible to find really good pieces of ordinary furniture on sale. Patsy and I furnished Bilbury Grange with a good many splendid pieces of furniture which we had bought at auctions and for which we had paid quite modest sums. Patchy, however, had once explained to me that the best and most exciting items are often the things which are sold at the end of an auction. These are usually assorted items which the auctioneer has dismissed as being of no great value. So, for example, a collection of old books may be dumped in a box and sold as 'box and contents'. (Sometimes, the box will be a rather nice old trunk or a useful wine crate rather than a boring cardboard box.) And garden equipment is usually left to the end of the auction and then sold without many people showing interest. Many of the buyers will have drifted off and those who are left will be in a hurry to pay their bills and claim their purchases. It's often easy to pick up garden statues, old benches and tools for very little money.

Anyway, I found the old sledge hammer, took it upstairs and handed it to Thumper who took hold of it as though he knew what he was doing which I'm sure he did.

Patsy and I both winced as he swung the head of the hammer against our bedroom wall. I confess that as he started his backswing, I began to have second thoughts about what we were doing but by then it was too late.

Moments later, we had a huge hole in our bedroom wall and it was clear that Thumper was correct.

Someone had covered up a large fireplace with a false wall made out of old boards.

As we all leant forward to see exactly what had been revealed, and what lay behind the boarding which the blow had shattered, we had the shock of our lives as a large bird flew out of the hole and started flying around the bedroom.

In the excitement of trying to find out whether or not we had a bedroom fireplace, I had completely forgotten that our interest in the wall had arisen because Patsy and I had heard something scrabbling and scratching behind it.

Within a minute, the bird had flown round the room at least five hundred times (I know that's an exaggeration but that's what it seemed like) and there was soot absolutely everywhere. The bird, poor thing, was so covered in ancient soot from the inside of the chimney, and was so frantic, that it was impossible to say exactly what it was. It could have been a crow, a rook, a magpie or a jackdaw. For a moment, I even thought that it could have been a pigeon. It could have been almost any medium to large sized bird though it wasn't big enough to be a seagull or a raven.

At that point Patsy screamed.

She did not scream because she was frightened (she is a farmer's daughter and does not scare easily) she screamed because the bird was turning our bedroom into a complete mess.

To be fair, I think that her response was fairly muted. Many women would, I suspect, have become overtly hysterical at the sight of a soot covered bird flying around a neat bedroom, depositing soot here, there and everywhere.

It is no exaggeration to say that within seconds the bed, the carpet, the curtains and all the furniture were covered in a layer of soot. We quickly discovered that a fairly modest amount of soot shares with blood and jam the capacity to cover a far larger area than might seem possible.

Our first task was to catch the bird.

This proved easier than expected since the bird's wings were heavily caked with soot and the creature was, therefore, slower in its movements than it might otherwise have been. Nevertheless, Patsy, Thumper and I spent several minutes diving around the bedroom before we caught it.

Modestly, I saw that 'we' caught it.

Surprisingly, perhaps, I was the one who eventually managed to grab the poor bird.

Realising that if I caught it in my hands there was a real risk that I might damage a wing, I caught the bird in a shirt I took from the laundry basket in the corner of the bedroom. Thumper had been using a towel and Patsy had been using a blouse; both items had been taken from the same laundry basket.

The bird was a crow and once I had it gently but firmly wrapped in the shirt, I carried it downstairs with Patsy and Thumper following closely behind. I took the 'parcel' to the kitchen and then through the back door into the garden.

The big question was what should we do with it next?

I was worried that if I let the bird go it would be vulnerable to predators.

'It'll be fine,' said Thumper. 'Just let it go and then stand back because there's going to be another cloud of soot!'

I unfastened the bundle, placed it on the ground and retreated in the way one does after lighting a firework.

Slowly, the crow emerged from the folds of the shirt. It looked a lot livelier than I had feared. It shook itself, fluttered its wings and produced a small cloud of soot. It then repeated the process several times. Each time it shook and fluttered, the cloud of soot was smaller.

'It'll be fine,' said Thumper. 'It'll go and have a wash in a minute.'

And sure enough, a minute or so later the bird walked about a little, fluttered into the air, came back to earth, tried again and then, delighted that everything seemed to be working satisfactorily, it took off and flew off towards our bird bath. Moments later it was splashing and fluttering and using its beak to clean and preen the remains of the soot from its wings. It was good to know that we'd succeeded in rescuing the bird though the price of the rescue had, perhaps, been a little higher than we might have liked.

'I suppose we'd better go back up and look at the damage,' sighed Patsy.

I could tell that she really didn't want to go back upstairs at all. I wasn't too keen either.

'I think you've got a pretty nice looking Victorian fireplace surround behind that board,' said Thumper, offering us hope that releasing the crow might leave us with something to be pleased about.

And he was right.

It took several hours to clear the sooty mess in the bedroom but there was a reward. When we had removed the partition which had been put up, we unearthed a magnificent, Victorian hearth with a surround consisting of beautiful and largely undamaged tiles. Whoever had put up the partition had even left the cast iron dogs in place inside the fireplace. The fireplace was full of twigs and it was clear that several nests must have been built in the chimney over the years.

'I have no idea why they built the partition wall across the whole of one side of the bedroom. It was a very solid affair, constructed out of real wooden boards. Patsy and I had rather hoped that we might find something valuable hidden in what would have been the two recesses if only the fireplace itself had been boarded up.

But we didn't find anything valuable.

There was nothing there but a large pile of old magazines and newspapers from Edwardian times. The owners of the property must have been well read because there were copies of *The Times*, *The Morning Post* and *The Devon and Exeter Gazette*. There was also a huge pile of magazines such as *Punch, Illustrated London News* and *The Strand*. It was clear from the newspaper dates that the partition must have been put up in around 1909. Still, as Thumper remarked: it could have been worse; we could have discovered a couple of human skeletons sealed up behind the partition.

The serious downside was that, as a result of our breaking down the partition, we had to completely redecorate the bedroom.

One upside was that much of our bedroom was now two and a half feet longer than it had been before. I don't think anyone really objects to having their bedroom extended a little at no real cost to themselves.

And the other upside was that we had a file collection of several hundred old newspapers and magazines. Some people might have regarded this as a nuisance, just rubbish to be disposed of. Some might have simply carted them off to an auction house in the hope that the haul would produce enough of a profit to pay for the wallpaper we had to buy. But I'm afraid I kept them all and I'm still reading them. Indeed, I have to admit that I get far more pleasure out of reading newspapers and periodicals dated 1909 than I could possibly get from reading contemporary publications.

I don't know what happened to the crow after he'd cleaned himself off and flown away. But Patsy and I both felt we were in his debt and we still regard all crows with great affection.

The Student

At the entrance to the drive into Bilbury Grange there were two rather elderly gates; these were obviously much older than I was and considerably more distinguished and impressive looking.

We never shut the gates but they were oak and nicely made, with some rather fancy bits and pieces of carving, and Patsy and I thought they look rather splendid so when I noticed that some of the wood was beginning to show signs that it had been standing out in all weathers for many years without anyone paying it much attention, I bought a large tin of clear yacht varnish from Peter Marshall, who runs the village shop, and decided to give the gates a protective coating.

The label on the tin said that 'for best results four coats should be applied' but I didn't love the gates that much so I decided that one thick coat would do just as well.

'That's the stuff they paint on ocean going yachts,' Peter had assured me. 'I think they use it on the America's Cup contenders. The last four winners all used it so it must be good.'

I don't know how Peter knew any of this, and knowing him as well as I do I suspect it was all part of his sales patter, but it sounded convincing and it was reassuring so I believed him. We all tend to believe things we want to believe more readily than we believe things that we find unacceptable.

I was always telling myself to try to be more sceptical where Peter was concerned. After all, as Patchy Fogg once put it: 'If Peter had his way, the famous soliloquy from Mr Shakespeare's 'Hamlet' would read: 'To buy or not to buy, that is the question'.' Peter always did his best to convince his customers that buying something was the only sensible answer, whatever the question might have been.

Still, the varnish was clear and sticky and those seemed to me to be vital and admirable qualities in a varnish.

(It was Peter, incidentally, who once told me that William Shakespeare was a ruthless and sharp entrepreneur who made money by storing foodstuffs until there was a shortage and then selling them for huge profits. When Peter found this out he decided that Shakespeare was his hero. He also told me that the Bard was frequently summoned to court for failing to pay his taxes.)

I started to clean the gates at about nine o'clock one evening and since it was summer and the days were long, I honestly believed that I would be able to finish the job in the gloaming and be done long before it went too dark to see what I was doing.

It was, as Patsy pointed out later, a fairly silly time to start varnishing a pair of gates but I have never been put off doing sensible things at silly times or, has been pointed out on more than one occasion, doing silly things at sensible times.

I had not, however, allowed for the fact that Mrs Tempest would decide to go into labour at a few minutes before 10.00 and although she shells babies with an ease which makes professional assistance almost completely superfluous, both she and I would have considered it the height of bad manners if I hadn't been there, standing at forward short leg to take the catch, cut the cord and congratulate everyone concerned. (Her husband, who created this analogy, is a keen cricketer who plays for the Bilbury team.)

And, after the baby had been born, I'd had to drink a glass of malt whisky (from a bottle which they kept especially for my use on such occasions and can you think of a more splendid way to know that you're considered to be a proper 'family doctor'?) and take a couple of puffs from a cigar which her husband always insisted on giving to me because he knew that was what they always did in books and films. He knows that I don't usually smoke but he doesn't know, because I have never told him and I try to hide it, that the taste of a cigar makes me feel nauseous.

So, by the time I got back to Bilbury Grange it was dark and since there wasn't much of a moon the gates were just a blur in the night.

I tried to finish the varnishing but quickly found that I couldn't see (or remember) which bits I'd already done. I tried parking the Rolls Royce in such a way that by switching on the car headlights I could illuminate the work area. That would have worked, I think, if Patsy hadn't come out and reminded me that the lights on the Rolls Royce use a good deal of electricity and that when I'd once

116

accidentally left the lights switched on for an hour the battery had gone completely flat.

All of this explains why I was finishing off the varnishing at 8.30 a.m. the following morning and telling all the patients who arrived for the morning surgery that I would definitely be starting the surgery at 9.00 a.m. sharp and that I would make sure I washed all the varnish off my fingers.

'I don't want to have all my best bits varnished,' said Mrs Hardy with a laugh that drove the birds from the trees and startled Ben so much that she ran into the porch and hid behind the aspidistra that Patsy's mother gave us for our anniversary three years ago.

At ten minutes to nine, I narrowly avoided being run over as a sports car slid to a halt in the lane outside.

'Where can I find Bilbury Grange?' demanded the driver, a plump, red-faced young man in a sports jacket. I use the word 'demanded' advisedly. He wore an old school tie which I knew I ought to recognise and, sparkling in the early morning sunshine, a gold tiepin. If he had been admitted to prison the tiepin would be recorded as 'gold metal' but I was pretty confident it was gold. He looked like the sort of person to have the best and most expensive of everything. He doubtless had a silver spoon tucked away somewhere. He was wearing an expensive looking flat cap; the sort that you see a good deal of at point-to-point meetings throughout the English countryside.

'You've found it!' I told him, assuming that he was a visitor to the area who needed medical assistance. He certainly didn't look like a meter reader or an income tax collector.

He stared at the gate and then at me and then at the gate again. 'Is it worth it?' he asked. 'It looks a pretty old gate and a pretty boring job!'

'It's enormous fun and very satisfying,' I lied, suddenly remembering Tom Sawyer white- washing his Aunt's fence.

'Really?' He sounded very unconvinced.

'You can finish off what's left if you give me your apple core,' I told him.

'I beg your pardon?'

I repeated what I'd said.

'What apple core?'

'Or maybe just lend me your hat for an hour.'

He now looked at me as if I was an escaped lunatic.

'Tom Sawyer,' I explained.

'Who?'

'Don't you know 'The Adventures of Tom Sawyer'? Have you never read the 'Adventures of Huckleberry Finn'?'

If I had suddenly started speaking Mandarin he could not possibly have stared at me in more confusion.

'Mark Twain?' I suggested.

'Sorry, no, doesn't ring a bell,' he said.

I was, to be honest rather shocked that the visitor, whoever he was and whatever he wanted, had never heard of Tom Sawyer or Mark Twain and it seemed rather sad.

The famous Twain story of Sawyer and the fence painting had popped into my mind because my chum Patchy Fogg, a local antiques dealer, had recently acquired a very old typewriter which he believed was one which Twain had owned. The typewriter, made by the 'Ohio MfgCo' was so old that the keyboard was arranged in the original, old-fashioned, straightforward abcdefhijk fashion rather than the more familiar qwertyuiop design (which was introduced to slow down typists who were typing too quickly and getting their keys all in a tangle.)

The keyboard on the old typewriter which Patchy had acquired was enormous for it had separate keys for all the capital letters and all the letters were on very long stalks. What made Patchy so excited was the fact that the machine had the letters SC neatly scratched on the base. Now Twain was, of course, one of the first people in the world to use a typewriter and his real name was Samuel Clemens. Patchy was completely convinced that the typewriter was genuine and a real collector's item. He was so convinced that it was an antique that he said he was going to keep it. 'I couldn't sell this,' he told me excitedly. 'It's the first real antique I've ever found!'

I had intended to embellish my comment about Mark Twain with this local story, but before I could say anything else the stranger had put his foot on the accelerator, sprayed me with gravel and swung into the driveway where he parked his tiny sports car in front of my Rolls Royce 20/25 – blocking me in completely.

Most of my patients know not to park in front of the Rolls Royce because if I have an emergency to attend to I always need to get out of the driveway quickly. It is for that reason that I always park the car facing the exit of the driveway. I moved to ask the driver to shift his car but I was too slow for he had disappeared into the house. Looking at my watch I realised that I had better finish the varnishing, go indoors, get cleaned up and put on a tie and a jacket if I intended to start the surgery on time.

Four minutes later I finished the varnishing, popped the sticky brush into the empty tin and headed for the house. The young man who had driven the sports car was waiting inside the hall. He was still young but he was now also clearly short and surprisingly chubby.

'Where can I find the doctor?' he demanded in the sort of tone that Victorian and Edwardian landowners used to favour when addressing the servants.

I looked at him and, with the hand holding the empty can and the paint brush, pointed to the room in which patients usually wait to be seen. 'The waiting room is in there,' I told him.

'No, you misunderstand,' he said. 'I'm not a patient. I'm Mr Munton.' He said this as if I should have recognised the name.

'Mr Munton?' I said, racking my brains and wondering why I was expected to know who Mr Munton might be.

'From Birmingham University,' he explained. 'I'm here as an observer.'

He made it sound as if he were visiting in an official capacity; to check up on me in some way.

'To observe what?'

He sighed with obvious exasperation. 'Just tell me where I can find the doctor?' he demanded, rather more brusquely this time. The tone had hardened into something that might be used with a recalcitrant and somewhat half-witted servant who needed putting in his place.

'I'm the doctor.'

He stared at me in astonishment. 'You're the doctor?'

'Yes. Can I help you?'

'I'm Franklin Munton,' he said. Foolishly I shook it, forgetting that my hand was still rather sticky with varnish.

And as he grimaced and reached into his pocket for a linen handkerchief (which, I didn't mind betting, was probably embroidered with his initials) I remembered who he was and why he was standing in the hall of Bilbury Grange.

A few months earlier I had received a telephone call from one of the lecturers at my old medical school in Birmingham. He told me that he was trying to arrange what he called 'one day professional experiences' for final year medical students.

'We're ringing up doctors who qualified here and asking if they would allow a student to sit in with them for a day. Just to observe what goes on. We think it might help the students make good, sound, career choices.'

Partly to get the lecturer off the phone, partly because the date he had offered was a long way away (and you can always kid yourself that the awful day will never arrive) I had agreed to take a student for the day.

I had also thought, I suppose, that I might be able to help a young doctor in the same way that Dr Brownlow had helped me when I had first entered general practice. At the back of my mind lay the thought that I might be able to offer a little guidance. Students at medical school are taught a great deal about glanders, the ague and the Black Death and quite probably botts disease too (though, come to think of it, I have a suspicion that is something which mainly afflicts sheep) but they are taught nothing very much about the sort of ailment commonly seen in a GP's surgery, where patients wander in suffering with butterflies in their stomachs and frogs in their throats and where attempts to heal them are too often complicated by the presence of unexpected flies in the ointment.

And this was the student I had agreed to allow into my surgery; my 'observer' for the day.

When I'd deposited the empty varnish tin and washed my hands (and the student had washed his hands too) I introduced him to Patsy and then to Miss Johnson, the venerable practice receptionist. I told Miss Johnson to advise patients that I had a medical student with me and that if they didn't want him to stay in the consulting room all they had to do was to tell her.

'If they'd rather you weren't there, you can pop out through the French windows,' I told him. 'That way it won't be embarrassing for you or the patient.'

'The patients aren't given that option at any of the hospitals attached to the medical school,' said Mr Munton, rather crossly.

'But that's what's going to happen here,' I told him. It did not seem to me too unreasonable that I should be allowed to set the house rules, since we were in my consulting room.

I too was now rather cross and beginning to regret the whole exercise. The day hadn't really got off to the best of starts. I had an awful suspicion that although the day had begun with some fairly common or garden pique it could well end up with more than its fair share of high dudgeon on display.

I showed Mr Munton a spare chair in my consulting room, put it up a corner so that he could sit quietly and out of the way and showed him the French windows through which he could make his escape if Miss Johnson told me that a patient who was coming in didn't want the student to stay in the room.

'I think it's probably best if you sit quietly,' I told him. 'If you have any questions or comments keep them until the patient has left.'

He said he would do this and took a smart leather notebook out of an outer jacket pocket and an expensive looking fountain pen from an inner pocket. The notebook, the pen and the bad-tempered scowl that seemed to be a fixture made him look like a traffic policeman. I felt it likely that no one had ever described him as a hypergelast or a cachinnator and made a mental note to put these words onto the next list of oddities I compiled with my pal William.

A minute or so later the first patient came in.

'It's his second attack of tonsils in eighteen months,' said Beryl Bussage before she'd even sat down. She sounded rather cross about it, as though she'd bought the tonsils in good faith and was now rather disappointed in their performance.

I told her small son Reginald to open his mouth wide so that I could take a look inside. His tonsils were certainly inflamed and swollen. I took a look at his medical records.

'The antibiotic did its job very well last time,' I said. 'I'll prescribe the same thing again.' I reached for my prescription pad and my pen.

I knew that most cases of tonsillitis went away without any treatment but an antibiotic helped to ensure that there weren't any complications. Besides, although I steadfastly refused to prescribe antibiotics for patients with colds or the flu (both caused by viruses which aren't affected by antibiotics), I didn't fancy being the first doctor in the world to tell a mother that I wasn't going to write out a prescription for an antibiotic for her child's tonsillitis.

'I want them taken out,' said Mrs Bussage firmly.

I looked at her.

'Most of the children in his class at school have had their tonsils taken out,' said Mrs Bussage. She sat back and folded her arms as though defying me to fail to agree that this was a sound argument for surgery.

'Surgeons used to rip out every child's tonsils,' I told her. 'The operation to remove the tonsils and another twin patch of lymphatic tissue called the adenoids was for years the most common surgical procedure performed. In some parts of the world a T and A operation – a tonsillectomy and adenoidectomy – was done as a routine when a child reached a certain age.'

'Well, there you are then, they must have known what they were doing,' said Mrs Bussage, with admirably misplaced faith in the medical profession.

'Ah, but doctors haven't always done sensible things,' I told her. 'Sadly, the history of medicine is littered with misconceptions, misapprehensions and misinterpretations and medical history is full of examples of doctors doing things or saying things which they later regretted and which have been proved pointless or dangerous or both. During the First World War, for example, it was argued that workers in gunpowder mills were made healthier by breathing in dust containing charcoal, sulphur and salt petre. At the same time, it was customary for doctors to chop out great lengths of bowel simply because they could and one or two eminent surgeons said it was a good idea to do so. Doctors used to bleed their patients because they thought it would help make them stronger. Lots of my predecessors used leeches. Surgeons removed bits of brain from patients who were mentally ill. Others gave their patients massive electric shocks. Patients who had syphilis were treated with mercury without anyone realising just how dangerous it was. In the 1920s, doctors regularly removed all of their patients' teeth to protect them from infections such as tuberculosis. You don't have to go very far back to find yourself in an era when doctors thought that smoking was good for people. Doctors enthusiastically recommended cigarettes to all their nervous patients and, in addition, to men who seemed to be a bit undersized and 'weedy'. By the 1950s, a few outspoken nutters were just beginning to claim that smoking was dangerous but most people thought the cranks were just being as silly as those who said that fatty foods were bad for you. When I was a small boy everyone 'knew' that fat was good for you and that dripping spread on bread was as healthy a meal as, well, a sugar sandwich; and that both were as good for you as any meal any dietician or nutritionist could devise.'

I paused.

Mrs Bussage did not look convinced by anything I'd said.

'There are fashions in medicine,' I concluded, 'just as much as there are fashions in anything else. And it was, for quite a while, fashionable to remove the tonsils!'

My eye caught Mr Munton, sitting quietly in a corner. He looked shocked at my gentle criticisms of the medical profession.

'Well,' said Mrs Bussage. 'All that is as maybe but all I'm saying is that I think you should arrange for Reginald to have his tonsils taken out.'

'Let me tell you four things,' I said. 'And then if you still agree that Reginald should have an operation I will refer him to a surgeon.'

'First, the tonsils are there for a purpose. They aren't just a nuisance. They are the first line of the throat's defences in catching infections and preventing them going deeper into the body. If the tonsils are removed then they can't swell up but the infection might go deeper into the body and cause other problems.'

'Second, surgeons used to remove swollen tonsils because they had no other way of treating them. Today, we have penicillin and most of the time it is a drug which really works at curing tonsillitis.'

'Third, there is a risk with any operation. There is, for example, the risk of having an anaesthetic. If an operation is life-saving then the risk is usually worth taking. But Reginald's tonsils are not threatening his life. What a tragedy it would be if we arranged for an operation which he didn't really need and something terrible happened.'

And fourth, there is no doubt that removing the tonsils is still a fashionable operation. It is something doctors arrange because they think it ought to be done. In New York City, a group of American doctors examined 1,000 schoolchildren to decide whether or not they needed an operation to remove their tonsils. None of the children was ill. They were healthy, normal children. The team of doctors recommended that 61% of the children should have their tonsils removed. The remaining children were then examined by a second group of physicians. These doctors examined the children who were left and decided that 45% of these children needed to have their tonsils removed. A third set of doctors then examined the fairly small group of children who were left and these doctors recommend that 46% should have their tonsils removed. Finally, a fourth examination was made of the minute number of children who remained. On this occasion another 45% of the children were told that they needed to have their tonsils removed. At this point in the experiment just 65 children of the original 1,000 remained. The four groups of doctors had between them decided that 935 children needed to have their tonsils removed.'

Mrs Bussage reached out and took hold of Reginald. She put her arm around him. 'I didn't know there were any risks with the operation!'

'There are always risks with an operation,' I told her. 'If the operation is vital then the risks will be worth taking. But...'

I didn't get to finish the sentence.

'Does he have to have the operation?' asked Mrs Bussage. 'Can't you just give him more of those antibiotics that cured him last time?'

I said I thought that would be a good idea. 'If he gets a good deal of trouble with his tonsils we can always think again,' I told her. 'If we all think it's necessary for him to have the operation then I'll certainly fix it up.'

'Oh, I think we're a long way from that point, don't you, doctor?' said Mrs Bussage.

I wrote out a prescription and told her to give it to Patsy or Miss Johnson who would turn the prescription into medicine.

'Golly,' said Mr Munton, when Mrs Bussage and young Reginald had gone. 'You were a bit tough on the medical profession weren't you?' He clearly disapproved.

'I wanted to make a point,' I explained. 'And I thought it was important to help Mrs Bussage understand that medicine can sometimes get things wrong.'

'You certainly did that. Do you dispense your own medicines?'

'Yes. Otherwise it's a long way to the nearest pharmacy and many of my patients don't have cars or even bicycles.'

'Aren't there any buses?'

I smiled. 'If you relied on the buses around here you'd probably never go anywhere. And if you did manage to go somewhere you'd have a hell of a long wait before you get back.'

'Is it profitable?'

'Is what profitable? The bus service?'

'No. Is it profitable to run your own dispensary?'

I was puzzled. Naively, I hadn't ever thought about this. 'I wouldn't think so,' I replied. 'But I think it probably pays for itself so it doesn't actually cost us anything.'

Mr Munton looked at me as if I were mad. I got the feeling that the suspicions which he had harboured when he saw me varnishing our gate had been crystallised.

Mrs Ermintrude Trump was my next patient.

'I've got swollen knees,' she said, before she'd sat down. She pulled up her dress and showed me her knees. They certainly were swollen. She then turned and showed Mr Munton, to whom I had, of course, introduced her.

'Have you been doing a lot of praying or housework?' I asked her.

She laughed. 'I've probably not done as much praying as I should have done,' she admitted. 'But I've been giving the house a good spring-clean and nothing cleans a floor like a bit of old-fashioned elbow grease.'

'It looks as if you've got housemaid's knee,' I told her. 'If you'd been doing too much praying then you'd have parson's knee.'

She wasn't wearing stockings so I could easily examine her knees. It wasn't difficult to see that there was some fluid on both knees. When human knees spend a lot of time in contact with hard surfaces there is a tendency for the skin to get squashed and stretched and as a result a bursa develops. I told her this.

'My niece is a bursar in a school in Surrey,' said Mrs Trump, frowning.

'That's a b-u-r-s-a-r,' I explained. 'What you've got is a b-u-r-s-a.'

'And what is it?' asked Mrs Trump. 'It feels all squishy. Why is it squishy?'

'It feels squishy because it is squishy. It's just some fluid that has collected as a protective mechanism – to protect your knees. It can happen to other parts of the body too. Students and scholars sometimes get student's elbow. And believe it or not there used to be a condition known as weaver's bottom which affected weavers who spent a lot of time sitting down at their looms.'

'Oh I don't think I'll get that!' said Mrs Thump with a loud, throaty laugh. Her whole body shook when she laughed. 'I've got far too much fat on my bottom. So, doctor, what can I do about my housemaid's knee?'

'Have you finished your spring cleaning?'

'I certainly have! My floors are spotless.'

'Then I don't think either of us needs to do anything about it. The fluid will slowly disappear and so will the swelling. If it hasn't gone in a couple of weeks come and see me again and I'll fix you up with an appointment to see a surgeon at the hospital. He'll put a needle into the swellings and remove the fluid. But I don't think it will come to that.'

'That's an unusual name, isn't it?' asked Mr Munton when Mrs Trump had gone.

'Oh I don't think so,' I replied. 'There are quite a few Trumps about in this part of the world. There's a family of them in a hamlet called Churchill Barton. I suppose it's fair to call it a hamlet. Someone told me that officially a hamlet is a village without a church and there's certainly no church in Churchill Barton.' I thought for a moment. 'Come to think of it I think just about everyone living in Churchill Barton is called Trump.'

'I meant Ermintrude,' said Mr Munton.

'Oh no, that's not an unusual name. I know of three Ermintrudes in our village. It used to be a very popular name. It's usually shortened to Emma or Emmy but Mrs Trump doesn't like her name being abbreviated.'

'Living here must be like living in another century,' said Mr Munton with a quiet sigh.

It was, I thought, a sign of disapproval and disdain. I got the clear impression that Mr Munton was not a great fan of country life.

'I think you're probably right!' I said. 'But we like to think that we are tiptoeing gently towards the front edges of the 20th century. Working in a village community is very different to working in a town or a city. The environment is different, the relationships are different and, of course, there is a greater sense of community here than you will ever find in places such as Birmingham or London.'

Mr Munton took the top off his fountain pen and wrote something down in his notebook. I assumed that his tutor had told him to write a report on his impressions of a country doctor working in a practice in Devon. When he'd finished writing he looked at it, thought for a moment and then underlined it with his pen. Maybe, I thought, I was getting through to Mr Munton. Maybe he might learn one or two things after all.

'I've just remembered I've got to telephone a chap I play squash with,' he explained, when he saw me looking at his notebook to see if he'd finished writing. 'I had a game fixed for this evening but I'll have to reschedule it.'

I always like to learn something new every day but I rather got the feeling that Mr Munton felt that he was already full to the brim with all the knowledge he was likely to need in life. I, on the other hand, had reached the age when I was far more aware of the things I didn't understand than the things I knew. I still struggled to explain to myself why the cap doesn't stick when you put it back onto the open end of a tube of glue. It occurred to me that Mr Munton was perhaps not mature enough to have acquired an interest in people. Or maybe he was so concerned with himself, and his own narrow world, that he would never be interested in the wider world.

Dottie McTavish, may have had a Scottish sounding name but as far as I know, she had never been as far north as Bristol, let alone Glasgow or Edinburgh and she was as English as it is possible to imagine anyone to be.

Miss McTavish was 14, gracile, daphlean and leesome and before she came into the surgery, I had ushered Mr Munton out through the French windows.

I had no idea whether or not Miss McTavish would have consented to my having a medical student in the consulting room but I had never met a girl between the ages of 12 and 16 who wasn't shyer than she liked people to know.

'Miss Johnson said you had a student with you,' said Miss McTavish, looking around.

I'd watched her grow up from a small, freckly gamine with a penchant for climbing trees and playing cowboys and Indians (both activities leading to regular scrapes and grazes but, fortunately, nothing more substantial) into the early makings of a beautiful, young woman; caterpillar into butterfly. She had red hair and green eyes and would soon be leaving broken hearts strewn behind her like rose petals after a summer wind.

'He's popped out. And he won't be coming back in while you're here.'

'Oh!' she said. I could see the relief. It was almost tangible.

'What's the problem?'

'I've got a lump,' she whispered. 'I think I've got cancer.'

'Where is it?'

'Just here!' She touched her side, at the bottom of her rib cage. 'It feels hard.'

'How long has it been there?'

'I only found it last night; when I was getting ready for bed.'

I gave thanks, for the umpteenth time, that I did not have an appointments system which meant that patients had to wait a week, a fortnight or a month to see a doctor in order to share a concern.

It occurred to me that if she'd been a couple of years older I would have suspected that a boyfriend had found it for her. Spouses, partners and lovers are often the one to find a physical abnormality.

'Pull up your blouse and let me look.'

Blushing, she stood up and pulled her blouse out of her skirt.

'Now show me. Where is the lump?'

She put her finger on it. 'Just here.'

I examined her and then told her she could pull down her blouse. She did so and then sat down.

'You haven't got cancer,' I told her immediately. 'You haven't got anything wrong with you. Your lump is perfectly normal and healthy.'

They probably heard her sigh of relief in distant parts of Cornwall.

'It's a rib,' I told her. 'It's been there all your life but you never noticed it before.'

'But it doesn't seem attached to anything!'

'Well it's attached to your spine at one end but it's not attached to your sternum, your breastbone, or to any of the other ribs. So it seems to be loose at the front – it's sometimes called a floating rib. Lots of people have them.'

'I feel a fool!' she said, and she did look embarrassed.

'Why on earth do you feel a fool?'

'Just finding a rib that I'd never noticed before!'

'It happens often. You're not foolish.'

'And it's not anything to worry about?'

'Absolutely not! It is perfectly healthy and it's not in the slightest bit dangerous.'

She stood up, beaming. 'That's such a relief, doctor!' She moved towards the door and then turned back for a moment. 'Thank you for sending the student out,' she whispered. 'I'd have felt even more of a fool if someone else had been in the room.'

When she'd gone I went to the French windows and called Mr Munton back into the consulting room. I was glad I'd sent him out when Miss McTavish had been in the surgery.

He had, he told me, been watching some young squirrels playing on the lawn.

'They look like rats with bushy tails!' he said.

'They do. But they don't behave in the slightest bit like rats. Rats are aggressive and greedy but squirrels are nervous, gentle and playful.'

'Well, they still look like hairy rats to me.'

My next patient, Amelia Cartwright, had hurt her arm.

'Have I broken it, doctor?' she wanted to know. She rolled up the sleeve of her cardigan and held out the arm for inspection

It didn't take more than a couple of moments to confirm that she hadn't broken anything.

'Did you fall?' I asked her.

She looked rather embarrassed.

'I fell off a space hopper.'

'Ah!' I said, as if this was entirely predictable. I had heard of space hoppers for they were at the time, all the rage. I had seen pictures in newspapers and magazines of children bouncing about on board brightly coloured, plastic 'hoppers'.

In reality, this had not been top of my list of possible causes of Mrs Cartwright's injury. It had occurred to me that she might have tripped or slipped on a loose rug but it had not occurred to me that she might have fallen off a space hopper.

Mrs Cartwright was in her 70s and not, perhaps, the prime target market for space hopping.

'I was doing quite well but suddenly I overbalanced,' she said. 'I think I got a bit over-confident.'

'What on earth were you doing on a space hopper?'

'My grandson wanted to try one and so he had his fifteen minutes on it and then he wanted to see his gran having a go. So I bought my fifteen minutes and had a go to please him.'

'What do you mean by you bought your fifteen minutes?'

'Oh Peter is renting them out,' said Mrs Cartwright. 'He's only managed to get hold of two and I've no doubt that he's realised he can make more money out of them by renting rather than selling them.'

I thought that sounded like Peter Marshall. I also thought it showed his entrepreneurial instinct to the full. Who else but Peter would have thought of renting out space hoppers for fifteen minutes at a time?

Peter Marshall, who runs the village shop and is rumoured by Thumper Robinson to have run it since the days when Alfred the Great was busy burning cakes, always claims that he makes a real effort to keep up with the times. 'You have to face the changes head on,' he says. 'You have to embrace new trends so that you can conquer them!'

And although it has been argued by some that Peter is usually a year or so behind the times with new ideas, he does usually get there in the end. Peter Marshall's village shop is the Bilbury department store; stacked to the rafters with turnips, drain cleaner, potatoes, dog food, tinned pears, tap washers, yacht varnish and a cornucopia of very useful stuff that you never know you want until you suddenly find you need it and can't manage without it.

Peter did not start selling plastic hula hoops until the mid-1960s when they had been largely abandoned in England's larger towns and cities – though this lengthy delay may have been as much a result of his enthusiasm for buying cheaper products, and waiting for over-stocks to become available at the warehouse than a failure of awareness. There is no doubt that when hula hoops did finally appear in Bilbury, they had been bought by Peter at a wholesale price which reflected their fall in popularity elsewhere in the country. Naturally, the retail price did not fall in a similar way. No one would have expected it to do so.

With space hoppers it was different. Peter had managed to get hold of two of them right at the height of the craze.

'Could I have a bandage, do you think?' asked Mrs Cartwright.

'I don't think…' I began.

'I know it doesn't really need one,' said Mrs Cartwright. 'But my grandson is staying with me for a few days while his parents have gone to Cornwall. To be honest, he's wearing me out and he wants to go back for another go on the space hopper tomorrow. If I have a bandage on one arm it might give me an excuse to take it a bit easier for a day or so. I can just stand there and offer him encouragement.'

I got up, fetched a bandage from a drawer and started to wrap it around Mrs Cartwright's arm. 'Tell him he can have your fifteen minutes on the space hopper as well as his own,' I suggested. 'He'll be thrilled by that and so not too disappointed that you're not having another go.'

'What a splendid idea!' said Mrs Cartwright beaming.

I finished the bandaging and fixed it all in place with a safety pin and lots of impressive looking strapping.

When Mrs Cartwright left she was quite content.

'Another satisfied customer!' I said to Mr Munton.

'It's not exactly proper medicine, is it?' said Mr Munton, who was a little uppity for my taste.

It occurred to me that our relationship (such as it was) had never acquired the essential ingredient of respect which is pretty much a standard requirement for the pupil-teacher association. I did wonder if perhaps things had been marred by the fact that Mr Munton still thought of me as a gate-varnisher rather than a man of medicine. Or, more likely, it was my fault. It takes special skills and an unusual type of patience to be a teacher. The truth is that my hands were full looking after my practice and I had neither the time nor the inclination to acquire teaching skills.

Mrs Isabel Outhout had been a patient of mine since I had taken over the practice from Dr Brownlow. And before that she had been a patient of Dr Brownlow's. She was a nervous, shy woman in her mid-30s who hurried everywhere she went. An inch short of five feet tall and weighing less than seven stones she always wore long Victorian dresses together with old-fashioned button up ankle boots and a shawl.

On reflection, I am sure that Mrs Outhout was the only woman under 60 whom I had ever seen use a shawl and she wore one all the time; summer and winter. It certainly seemed to be a useful and versatile piece of clothing. In the winter she wore a thick, woollen shawl which she used as a coat, scarf and hat and in the summer she wore a thin, silken one which she used to shade her face and neck from the sun. She had jet black hair and brown eyes but was terrified of burning in the hot weather. Her skin was as white as paper and she wanted to keep it that way. Her husband was called Dwayne Outhout.

The Outhouts lived in Bilbury but Isabel Outhout worked in Barnstaple, where she was a shop assistant in an old-fashioned millinery and haberdashery store. The bus service in North Devon was woeful and she couldn't afford a car so she travelled between Bilbury and Barnstaple on a 50cc Honda moped. There were no rules about helmets in those days and she rode her moped flat out with her hair flying free in the wind behind her. She once told me, with some pride, that she regularly hit 28 mph on the downhill stretches, though she admitted that she managed considerably less on the uphill stretches. When it rained she carried a clear umbrella, jamming the handle between her left arm and her chest so that she could keep both hands on the controls. It was one of the strangest sights I've ever seen but it was apparently extremely effective at keeping her relatively dry. I saw her once come back from Barnstaple in a snow storm. It was a sight I shall never forget. The moped, the umbrella and Mrs Outhout were all white and apart from the phut phut phut of the moped engine, it appeared as though a strangely angelic ghost were riding along the lane.

'I'm terribly worried, doctor,' Mrs Outhout told me, settling down and adjusting her shawl. 'I had to see a doctor while I was on holiday in London. Dwayne and I went up to have a week doing the sights: the Tower of London, Buckingham Palace, Madame Tussauds and so on. While we were there, I developed an ear infection. The doctor the hotel recommended gave me some antibiotics which have cleared up the infection, thank heavens because it was very painful, but he insisted on doing some blood tests. He said he thought I had a thyroid problem.'

'Did he say why he thought that?'

'He said that being thin and very nervous are well-known signs of thyrotoxicosis.'

'They are,' I agreed. I didn't bother to mention, however, that lots of people are thin and nervous without having anything wrong with their thyroid glands.

'I had to go and see him after five days and he told me that according to the results from the laboratory, I have something called euthyroid.'

I frowned, slightly confused. 'What exactly did he say? Can you remember his precise words?' I looked at her husband who had accompanied her into the surgery.

'He said the tests showed that Isabel was euthyroid,' replied Dwayne. He took a small diary out of his pocket and showed me the word 'euthyroid' written on the back inside cover. 'I asked him how to spell it,' added Mr Outhout.

'Did he tell you what it meant?'

'No,' said Mr Outhout.

Mrs Outhout shook her head, agreeing with her husband.

'Did he tell you that you needed to come and see me?'

'No. He didn't say anything about any more treatment,' said Mrs Outhout. 'But when he said that I was euthyroid I thought I'd better come and see you as soon as I could.'

I started to say something but Mr Outhout talked over me. He wasn't being rude. He was simply desperate to explain to me how urgently he thought his wife's condition should be treated.

'We've been worried sick since we had the diagnosis,' said Mr Outhout. 'We cut our holiday short and came home because Isabel wanted to talk to you about it. We wanted to make sure we started any treatment as quickly as possible.'

'Does it need an operation?' asked Mrs Outhout. There were tears in her eyes. 'I don't think I could bear going into hospital for an operation. I don't know why but I do worry so. My mother was in hospital for six weeks before she died and it affected me quite a lot.'

'We have some money saved for a rainy day,' said Mr Outhout. 'We can pay for private treatment if it would help; if it would speed things up or help us find a better surgeon.'

I held up a hand in an attempt to silence them both. 'There's nothing wrong with your thyroid gland,' I told Mrs Outhout.

'We could travel to Exeter or Bristol if you thought it necessary,' said Mr Outhout.

I repeated what I'd just said.

The two of them heard me this time and were clearly stunned for they were silent for a moment or two.

'How do you know?' demanded Mrs Outhout.

'The doctor in London did the tests and said Isabel was euthyroid,' said Mr Outhout. 'Surely that must mean that something is wrong.'

'It means exactly the opposite of that,' I told him. 'The word 'euthyroid' is just a medical term for 'normal'.'

They both stared at me, disbelievingly.

I stood up, walked over to the bookcase where I keep most of my medical books and pulled out a large, medical dictionary. I flicked through the pages until I came to the word 'euthyroid' and showed it to them both.

'It says that euthyroid means having a normally functioning thyroid gland,' said Mr Outhout, having read from my book. He looked at his wife, then reached out and took her hand.

He was the first one to start to cry.

And then she too started crying.

I pushed the box of paper handkerchiefs across my desk.

To be honest, just seeing them cry made me want to cry too.

'That's such a relief,' said Mr Outhout eventually.

'We've been worried sick,' said Mrs Outhout. 'We thought perhaps it was some sort of cancer of the thyroid gland.'

'It means there's absolutely nothing wrong with your thyroid gland!' I repeated.

There were then a few more tears and a bit of a cuddle before they stood up to leave.

'What a stupid doctor that man was!' said Mrs Outhout, pausing on her way out of the surgery. 'He made our lives miserable.'

'It doesn't matter love,' said Mr Outhout.

At that moment he was merely relieved that his wife was not ill. I suspected that he might feel differently a little later on.

'And he ruined our holiday!' Mrs Outhout pointed out.

I did not say anything. Doctors aren't supposed to criticise individual doctors – though I've always felt it's fair enough to criticise the profession as a whole when things are done badly.

But privately I had to agree with Mrs Outhout. Some doctors are so addicted to using posh words that they forget that not everyone understands medical terminology.

When they'd gone I looked across at young Mr Munton. He looked a trifle uncomfortable and I guessed that he too had never come across the word 'euthyroid'. But I knew he wouldn't say anything.

'They're a nice couple,' I said. 'It seems so unfair that their holiday was spoilt. I happen to know they'd been saving up for that trip for a year.'

'Well, at least she knows now that there's nothing wrong with her,' said Mr Munton with a rather careless shrug.

I really didn't like Mr Munton very much. He didn't seem to be overfilled with empathy; something which I have always felt is an essential quality for a doctor.

The next patient was Buxton Longwoody.

Mr Longwoody was 92-years-old and physically he was not in bad condition. If he'd been a car he would have been advertised as being 'in good running order'. He lived about three quarters of a mile away from Bilbury Grange but he always walked to the surgery and he always walked back again afterwards. Whenever I offered him a lift home he always declined; very graciously explaining that he enjoyed the exercise. Nevertheless, he did wobble a little and I always found that watching him set off towards home was always a little worrying. Miss Johnson always telephoned his neighbour around thirty minutes after he had left the surgery, just to make sure that he'd managed to get home safely.

His problem was that his memory was not what it had been when he'd been younger. He couldn't always remember precisely what he'd done the day before, though he could remember a good deal about things which had happened earlier in his life. He left school at 14 (his parents took him out of school, arguing that since he had learned how to read and write there wasn't much point in his staying on) and as a boy he had joined the army and he had travelled all over Africa in his country's service. He had risen through the ranks and when he left the army, he had attained the rank of Captain.

During the Second World War, he tried desperately to enlist so that he could serve again but after numerous rejections (on the basis of his age) he became a keen and vital member of the Civil Defence force. After the end of the Second World War, he decided he needed an interest and so he taught himself Greek. He learned the language well enough to read *Plutarch* in the original.

Mr Longwoody's memory was now so poor that when I gave him instructions of any kind I had to write them down on a piece of paper and pop the piece of paper into his left hand jacket pocket. Mrs Barker, his neighbour, called in every morning and every evening to check on him and when he had been to the surgery she always used to look for the piece of paper so that she could see what pills he needed to take or stop taking. We had tried giving Mr Longwoody the note to take charge of but he usually managed to lose it. Mrs Barker, the Good Samaritan, used to put a note in that same pocket if she wanted to tell me anything about her neighbour.

Despite his poor memory, he always took a keen interest in his surroundings and on his walks to and from Bilbury Grange he would often simply stand, look around and enjoy the countryside. There was no doubt in my mind that he got great pleasure from his walks through the village.

As an aside, I sometimes wondered why dementia had become so common, and seemed to be getting commoner. Some of it, I knew, was caused by tranquillisers, sleeping tablets, sedatives and so on – all of which can cause a real sense of confusion as well as memory loss. Some of the increase in the incidence of dementia was a result of doctors being more aware of the problem, and diagnosing it more frequently. But I couldn't help wondering if some of it might not be environmental. I remember having the thought that toxins in our world, in the air, in our food or in our drinking water, might be damaging our brains.

But I could never avoid the suspicion that part of the problem was that a generation or two ago older citizens were looked after by their families. When those older folk became forgetful and confused it didn't matter too much because there was always someone around to look after them; to make sure that they ate, drank, exercised, rested and came to no harm. By the 1970s, family units had broken down and the elderly were often living alone, relying on neighbours rather than relatives. And so the problem of dementia became more apparent.

It wasn't always easy to do but I tried to make sure that Mr Longwoody only ever needed to take tablets in the morning and in the evening so that his neighbour, the Good Samaritan, could supervise the tablet taking and make sure he took precisely what had been prescribed and nothing more or less.

When Mr Longwoody had sat down, I introduced him to Mr Munton, something I was careful to do with all my patients that morning.

'Did you have a good walk here?' I asked.

'Splendid!' he replied crisply. 'I saw half a dozen rabbits, a squirrel and a hen partridge. And a pair of busy blackbirds racing about getting food for their young.'

'Any butterflies?'

Mr Longwoody had always been keen on butterflies and knew a good deal about them

'Not one,' he replied rather sadly. 'They should be around by now. Maybe I'll see some on my way home.'

I asked him if he had anything for me. Sometimes he remembered he had a note for me. Sometimes he had to be reminded. And sometimes I had to ask his permission and dip my hand into his pocket myself to retrieve the note.

He frowned in thought.

'Do you have a note for me from Mrs Barker?' I suggested, offering the question as a hint. 'It might be in your jacket pocket.'

Mr Longwoody stuck his right hand in his jacket pocket and produced a neatly folded square of blue Basildon Bond writing paper. He handed the paper to me with a slightly guilty smile. He still had all his teeth and they looked to be in fine condition. 'Sorry, doctor,' he said. 'I nearly forgot. Damned memory of mine gets worse every day. I'd forget my head if it wasn't nailed on. Mrs Barker asked me to give you this.' He handed me the note which I unfolded and read.

This is what it said:

'Mr Longwoody has been eating well but his varicose eczema is playing up a little. He won't talk to me about it but he always goes to bed much earlier than we do and I've seen the lights go on in his cottage at midnight or even later so I think his prostate is still playing up. I worry about this because he has to walk across the landing and pass the stairs to get to his bathroom. As you know, he is a bit wobbly. If you approve and can persuade Mr Longwoody that it's a good idea, I'll ask Thumper Robinson to pop round and

put a wooden gate at the top of the stairs. He needs some more of his blood pressure pills. Thank you (signed) Daphne Barker.'

'I hear you're having to get up several times in the night,' I said, putting down the note.

'Just to go to the lavatory,' said Mr Longwoody. 'The bladder doesn't seem to hold so much fluid these days. Or maybe it's that gland thing. What's it called?'

'The prostate gland. It tends to get larger with age – and that can cause problems. I examined you last time you were here and yours is bigger than it should be but it's nothing to worry about and I wouldn't recommend an operation. But I'm worried about you walking along your landing at night. Will you let Thumper put a gate at the top of your staircase?'

'A gate? What for?'

'It would stop you falling down the stairs when you get up to go to the toilet in the middle of the night.'

'Ah, that's a good idea,' said Mr Longwoody. 'But how will I get downstairs in the mornings?'

'The gate will have a catch and a spring,' I said. 'When you want to go downstairs you just open the gate. But if you fall against the gate it will stop you going down the stairs involuntarily.'

'Oh yes, that's a splendid idea! Will you arrange that or shall I?'

'Thumper Robinson will do it for you.'

'Oh fine. I know Thumper. He's a good, reliable lad. I'd have liked to have had him with me in Africa.'

I couldn't help smiling. The idea of Thumper Robinson serving in any army was quite a thought. Thumper is not someone who regards discipline as a 'good thing'.

'I'll ask Mrs Barker to fix it up,' I told him.

'What about the cost?' asked Mr Longwoody. 'Shall I settle up with you now?'

'No, no,' I said. 'There won't be any charge. The NHS will provide the gate for you.'

I checked Mr Longwoody's blood pressure which was fine, checked his heart and lungs, which were in good condition and looked at his varicose eczema, which wasn't as bad as I'd feared. I told Mr Longwoody that I would prescribe some more cream for the eczema.

I then picked up the telephone and asked Miss Johnson to put another two packets of his blood pressure pills and a tube of steroid cream into Mr Longwoody's jacket pocket when he left. Finally, I wrote a reply to Mrs Barker and gave it to Mr Longwoody who put it into his jacket pocket.

He then stood up, we shook hands and he left.

'Will the NHS really pay to put a gate at the top of his stairs?' asked Mr Munton, when Mr Longwoody had left. This was the first time he had asked a question or, to be honest, shown any interest in the patients I had seen.

'I'm afraid I don't think they will – not that I know of anyway.'

'So how will you arrange to have it done? You did tell the old chap you'd fix it up for him.'

'Oh, it won't be a problem. I've got plenty of bits of suitable wood in our barn and my pal Thumper Robinson will put up the gate. Or a friend of mine who is an antiques dealer might have an old gate that we can use. Mr Longwoody lives on a small army pension and a state pension and I fear that even when put together his pensions don't leave anything over for luxuries such as safety gates.'

'Oh,' said Mr Munton. 'The old chap did seem a little wobbly. And quite senile. Didn't anyone come with him?'

'No. He walked here by himself. He always does; winter or summer. Last winter he came here when there was two feet of snow on the road.'

'But he's suffering from dementia isn't he? He's clearly a bit confused. Aren't you worried that he'll get lost or run over on the way home?'

'He'll be fine,' I said. 'And his freedom and independence are important to him. He enjoys walking along the lanes, looking at the flowers, watching the animals.'

'Don't you think the old fellow should be on a geriatric ward or in some sort of home where he could be looked after?'

'No. He enjoys life. His neighbour helps look after him. He pays another villager to do his cleaning and his washing. He goes down to the village shop and does his own shopping and he does his own cooking though his neighbour takes him some meals. There are quite a few keeping an eye on him and he manages surprisingly well. And he isn't 'the old fellow' or 'the old chap' he's Mr Longwoody.'

Mr Munton looked at me, slightly puzzled. 'In hospital all old people are referred to by their Christian names. It makes them feel more at home.'

'How do you know? Have you asked them?'

'Well, no, not personally I haven't. Of course, I haven't.'

'Calling people by their Christian names is a way of talking down to them,' I said. 'It's demeaning and it turns them into subordinates. Are patients in the teaching hospital encouraged to address the consultants by their Christian names?'

'No, of course they aren't!' he laughed. He seemed greatly amused by the very idea of an old lady calling her surgeon 'Freddie' or referring to the ear nose and throat specialist as 'Ernie'.

'So, why should it be acceptable the other way round?'

'Well, it's rather different, isn't it?'

'No, I don't think it is different.'

'But the old chap, sorry Mr Longwood, could get run over,' said Mr Munton, abandoning this discussion and going back to the danger of an old and slightly demented man living in his own home, walking along the lanes and living a fairly independent life. 'And if he does his own cooking he might burn himself.'

'His name is Longwoody,' I told young Mr Munton. 'And it is true that he might get run over or burn himself. But look at the alternatives. I really don't think he would be happy sitting on an incontinent pad in a plastic chair in a home for old folks. He had an amazing life and he's entitled to live it out in dignity and in the way that allows him to feel comfortable, at peace with himself and with the world. He's lucky, I suppose, to live in a village where people have time to care for one another.' I didn't mention it but even Peter Marshall helped Mr Longwoody whenever he could. And although Peter usually had his eye on the bottom line, he would never cheat his older customers by giving them rotten fruit or vegetables. I knew for a fact that if they were short of money he would knock a few pence off his prices.

'I never think of old people as having had 'interesting lives',' said Mr Munton with a half-hearted chuckle. 'They always just seem old. It's as though they've always been old.'

'Every old person I've ever met has had an interesting life,' I told him without exaggeration. 'When he was a boy, Mr Longwoody met Cecil Rhodes in Africa. He served for a while with Baden Powell and he also served with T.E.Lawrence. He has some amazing old photographs which were taken in Lawrence's cottage in Dorset. He remembers all those people very well and I've had some amazing conversations with him. Astonishingly, he was present when T.E.Lawrence saved Winston Churchill from an angry mob. He was in a group of soldiers who were inspected by Dwight D.Eisenhower.' I paused. 'To be honest, Mr Longwoody had enough adventures in his life to provide scripts for a string of war movies and for a long running soap opera.'

'Is that the Baden Powell who founded the boy scouts?'

'That's the one. He was also a General in the army.'

'I didn't know that,' said Mr Munton.

'Didn't they teach you about the Siege of Mafeking at school?'

'No, I don't think so. And I haven't heard of the other two you mentioned.'

'You've not heard of Lawrence of Arabia?'

'Oh yes, I've vaguely heard of him. Didn't he live in the 18th century or something?'

'Lawrence of Arabia was T.E.Lawrence. Mr Longwoody knew him well.'

'Oh, really?'

Mr Munton sounded very bored so I called for the next patient.

I was beginning to get the feeling that Mr Munton was not a young man whose heart was calling him towards a career in general practice. The one thing I know for certain is that no doctor can possibly make a decent family doctor unless he is interested in people. (It also helps, I suspect, if in addition he enjoys doing what he can to make their lives a little easier.)

After Mr Longwoody had set off on his journey home, I saw half a dozen patients who simply needed repeat prescriptions. Two or three patients needed to have their blood pressure checked. A couple of patients needed notes to confirm that they needed to stay off work for a little longer. And the last patient was a young woman called Ginny Whales.

Mrs Whales worked as a cashier and general assistant in a petrol station on the Lynton Road. Her husband was an AA patrolman who spent his days driving around the countryside rescuing stranded motorists, mending cars and helping people get on with their journeys. In those days a man with a screwdriver, a spanner and battery charging leads could solve most of the roadside problems he encountered. The couple lived in one of the cottages near Blackmoor Gate. Mr Whales grew prize winning carrots and Mrs Whales had the most extraordinary collection of small model lighthouses. I'd never done a formal count but Mrs Whales must have had 40 or 50 model lighthouses. They all appeared to be made out of granite. Some of the lighthouses had little clocks fitted into the granite and others had thermometers. Most had the name of the resort etched into the base. I remember that there were, among many others, 'A Present from Llandudno', 'A Present from Margate' and 'A Present from Torquay'. Some people collect old cars, some collect stamps, some collect Victorian photographs and Mrs Whales collected small, granite models of lighthouses and it is a good thing, is it not, that we are all different in our tastes and interests. If we all wanted to collect Victorian photographs then the prices would go through the roof and many collectors would be forever doomed to disappointment.

When I first saw all these little model lighthouses when visiting the Whales's home, I couldn't help thinking that they were the ugliest souvenirs I'd ever seen. And there were so many of them! They seemed to be on every available flat surface. I could understand someone receiving one as a gift from a friend or a relative and then putting it on display out of a sense of duty, but I couldn't help wondering why on earth anyone would deliberately collect so many of the darned things.

Indeed, it did occur to me that Mrs Whales had perhaps been given one of the things and had, out of politeness perhaps, foolishly thanked the donor rather too effusively before putting it out on display. Under these circumstances it is very easy for the donor to be convinced that the gift was more successful than it was. And so she (it is, I believe, usually women who are responsible for choosing souvenirs or small thank you gifts) buys another and before you know where you are the house is full of them. When there are two of these things sitting on the windowsill, it is easy for other relatives and friends to suspect that they have spotted an answer to their present buying dilemmas. Instead of buying bath salts, talcum powder or toilet roll covers made in the shape of Spanish dancers, the well-informed friends and relatives hunt for, buy and bring back small model lighthouses which appear to be made out of granite and which have little clocks or thermometers built into them – and the name of the resort engraved on the base. They do this out of kindness, of course. I had a patient who had a massive collection of small elephants. She confessed to me one day that she absolutely hated them all but that it was far too late to throw them out or to stop new ones coming.

I am forever grateful that I kept these thoughts to myself, and did not make a joke or a clever remark about the collection, for it quickly became apparent that, apart from a few which had been purchased for her by her husband, Mrs Whales had bought all the little lighthouses herself. She and I would have been forever embarrassed if I had made the tactless remark which had been sitting on the top of my tongue ready to be dispatched into the world. Moreover, she told me that she continued to collect them despite the fact that most of her friends and relatives thought they were daft things to collect. 'I'm very determined,' she said, 'My mum always said I was very stubborn. Once I've decided to do something it would take an Act of God to change my mind.'

A year ago, Mrs Whales had her second baby and, as with the first child, which had been born a couple of years earlier, she refused point blank to breast feed the baby.

Rather surprisingly for those days, Mr and Mrs Whales were, pacing their family. This really was relatively unusual in Bilbury at the time. Other young wives in the village simply had a sequence of babies, producing them with great efficiency and very little fuss.

Indeed, in those pre-sex education days, it was not uncommon for young unmarried girls to find themselves in the same situation. Contraception was still something of a hit and miss affair and there were more than a few sad stories told by girls who found themselves suddenly putting on a great deal of weight, not realising that they would lose it again in nine months' time. 'I didn't know he'd done it until he started to pull up his trousers and told me he had to go so that he could catch his bus,' was perhaps the most poignant summary of a romance that produced a permanent souvenir of the occasion.

When I pressed Mrs Whales for a reason for her reluctance to breast feed she said that she was worried that she might lose her figure.

'I don't want to have droopy boobs and nipples like chapel hat pegs,' she confessed. 'I'm only 26! My friend Elspeth breast fed her baby and now she's got boobs down to her waist. Her nipples point at the floor and are as big as thimbles! She can't wear a bikini and if she wears a posh frock and wants a bit of cleavage she has to wear a bra with enough wire in it to hold up that big bridge in San Francisco, what's it called, the Golden Gate Bridge.'

I tried to convince her of the value of breast feeding.

I patiently explained that the fluid which comes from the breast in the immediate aftermath of pregnancy, the colostrum, contains protective substances which help to guard the new born baby against infection. I explained that cows' milk, however it is formulated or presented, can never be as healthy for a baby as a mother's milk. In short, I tried to 'sell' the idea that 'breast is best'.

Mrs Whales's husband joined my campaign and he tried in vain to persuade her that he really didn't mind at all if her breasts changed in shape, size, position or all three.

But Mrs Whales was absolutely adamant.

And as she herself had confessed, she was a woman who, once she had made up her mind, could be very stubborn indeed.

For example, when her two children were born, she had made it very clear that she was a member of a substantial but overlooked minority of women who didn't want their husbands to be present at the births. 'I don't want him to see me sweating and with my hair all over the place and my make-up a complete mess,' she said. 'To be perfectly honest,' she had added, 'I'd really not be there myself. If I had a choice, I'd prefer to be a mile away having a pleasant, romantic dinner for two in a decent restaurant. But I don't suppose that's possible. I have to be there. He doesn't.'

Mrs Whales had brought her two young children to the surgery with her and it was the second baby who was the patient. He had a horrid rash on his face and was clearly in some distress.

'My mum says it's a milk allergy,' said Mrs Whales, who had clearly been crying.

'And she's right,' I said.

I explained that an allergy to cows' milk is quite common and that it affects as many as one in fifteen of all babies under the age of a year.

'Has he had any tummy problems?' I asked her.

'He's had diarrhoea, awful diarrhoea,' said Mrs Whales. 'Nothing else. Just the rash and the diarrhoea.'

'Then it's an allergy to the cows' milk,' I told her. 'I can prescribe a replacement milk that won't cause an allergy reaction.'

'My mum suggested that I try goats' milk. Do you think that would be a good idea?'

'No, I'm afraid not. Babies who are allergic to cows' milk are often allergic to goats' milk too. Just stick with the milk I'll prescribe.'

'Will he get better?'

'Very quickly. The rash will disappear and the diarrhoea will stop. I can give you some cream to ease the rash but it will go away anyway quite quickly once the cows' milk is stopped.'

'It's my fault, isn't it?' she said suddenly.

'What on earth do you mean?'

'If I'd fed him myself then he wouldn't be ill, would he?'

'Not unless you'd been drinking milk yourself.'

'Can I start breast feeding now?'

'I'm afraid it's a bit late now.'

Mrs Whales nodded.

'Please don't worry about it,' I told her. 'He'll be better very quickly. And he'll be absolutely fine.'

I wrote out the necessary prescription and told Mrs Whales to give it to Miss Johnson who would give her what she needed.

'We're going to have three and I've decided that with the next one I'm going to breast feed,' said Mrs Whales, as I handed over the prescription. She said this quite defiantly; as though it were something she had decided to do despite my advice.

'Splendid!' I said.

And I knew that if she had decided to breast feed her next baby then it would most certainly be breast fed.

There are, without doubt, times when stubbornness can be a virtue.

As the door closed behind Mrs Whales, who was my last patient of the morning, Patsy came into my consulting room carrying a tray upon which were two cups, a pot of tea, a bowl of sugar, a milk jug and a large plate of assorted biscuits.

'I thought you might need these!' my wife said, putting the tray down on my desk.

Mr Munton, who had been sitting quietly in the corner, brought his chair over and helped himself to tea and one of those biscuits which have the jam in the middle. Patsy perched on the edge of the desk.

'Hope you weren't too bored!' I said to Mr Munton.

'Bored? Oh not too much. It was rather dull in places, I suppose. There's no real drama in general practice is there? If there's a real problem I suppose you just pass the patient onto the experts in the local hospital.'

'Do you want to come with me when I do the home visits? You can see a few patients in their home environments. It's really the best way to get a feel for general practice.'

'Always remembering that it's much easier to find them on a nice sunny day than at 3.00 a.m. in the middle of a thunderstorm!' said Patsy with a light laugh. 'Especially if the patient lives at the end of a long, muddy farm track.'

Mr Munton looked at his watch. 'Oh, I'm afraid I think I'd better be getting back,' he said. 'I promised to meet my fiancée in Exeter. She's spending the morning with friends of her people. That's where we stayed last night. And then we're going straight up to London. We've got a party in Hampstead to go to this evening.'

'Fine,' I said.

To be honest I was relieved. I hadn't enjoyed having a stranger sitting in my surgery. It didn't feel right. And I didn't want him coming on my rounds with me. I know young doctors and medical students need to have a chance to see medicine 'in the raw' but there are family doctors who enjoy teaching and training young colleagues and I had already decided that I preferred to leave such work to them.

'You seem to be doing everything today!' said Mr Munton. 'The surgery and the home visits.'

'Well, there isn't anyone else to do them.'

Mr Munton thought for a moment, clearly considering something. 'So what days do you work and what days do you have free?'

Patsy looked at me and I looked at her.

'There isn't anyone else. There aren't any other partners,' I told him. 'This is a single handed practice.'

'But don't you have an arrangement with another local practice so that you can have some time off?'

'Oh no,' I said. 'The other local practices are too far away. And besides, the truth is that a doctor from outside would never be able to find some of my patients. A doctor from Lynton or Ilfracombe would be driving round all night if they tried to find some of the cottages in Bilbury. When I first came here it took me a couple of years to find my way round the village.'

'It doesn't seem big enough to be a village.'

I looked at him, a little confused.

'It seems more of a hamlet.'

'No, we have a pub and a shop and several churches so technically we're a village.'

'Is that so?'

'I believe so. As I mentioned earlier, a hamlet is a village without a church.'

'Really?' He sounded remarkably disinterested. 'And what do you do about the weekends? You surely aren't on call at the weekends as well as during the day and at night during the week!'

'Oh, yes, I'm on call at the weekends too.'

'All of the weekends?' He sounded astonished.

'All of them! There isn't anyone else to do them.'

'But if you want to go to a show in London? Or to a party?'

'We don't go to shows or first nights or to parties.'

'Mr Munton paled. The very idea of not having an endless row of neatly engraved cardboard invitations dropping through the letterbox obviously appalled him.

'So what do you do for entertainment?' he asked.

'We have each other,' said Patsy. 'My husband is always entertaining. Not long ago he managed to get himself stuck on the roof of the local public house wearing nothing but my fluffy dressing gown, a pair of wellington boots and some swimming goggles.' She laughed at the memory.

If I live to be 100, people will still be reminding me of the time when I got stuck on the roof of the Duck and Puddle wearing Patsy's dressing gown, a pair of wellington boots and some damned swimming goggles. At the time, it had all happened quite logically.

Mr Munton stared at her, obviously not sure whether she was joking.

'It's a long story,' she said.

'I was wearing a yellow sou'wester too,' I pointed out, as though this made a difference. 'But only because it was raining quite heavily at the time,' I added.

'And we have loads of videos and long playing records,' added Patsy. 'And my husband has put together a marvellous library so we're never short of books to read.'

'A library?' said Mr Munton, who obviously considered that an evening spent with a book would be an evening wasted.

'Isaac Asimov once wrote that a library is a spaceship that will take you to the ends of the universe,' I said. 'A time machine that can take you far into the past, a teacher who knows everything and a friend who can amuse and console.'

'Isaac who?' said Mr Munton, puzzled. 'I don't think I know the name.'

I was beginning to feel very old. Mr Munton, it seemed, had not heard of any of the people I'd mentioned.

'Isaac Asimov is a very successful American writer,' I pointed out. 'He's best known for his science fiction novels but he's also a professor of biochemistry.'

'Oh,' said Mr Munton, clearly unimpressed. 'But for holidays you must hire a locum from outside. How does the locum manage? How do you arrange things if you want to go abroad? Do you get someone local to chauffeur the locum around the village?'

'Oh no,' laughed Patsy. 'It's much simpler than that. We just don't have holidays!'

'To be honest I don't think the practice could afford a locum and a chauffeur,' I added.

Mr Munton looked at us both as if we were mad.

'And why would we want to go anywhere else?' I asked. 'It's beautiful here. We have a lovely house and a marvellous garden. All our friends are round here.'

'Besides,' Patsy added, 'we've got too many animals to look after to even think of going away.'

'There are local boarding kennels surely?'

'For dogs and cats,' said Patsy. 'But where could we take Cedric?'

'Who is Cedric?'

'Our pig.'

'You have a pig?'

If we'd said we had a pet Martian in a cupboard he couldn't have been more obviously surprised.

'Well he's not exactly our pig,' explained Patsy. 'He belongs to some very nice Americans who won him in a skittle competition at the Duck and Puddle.'

Mr Munton looked at us as if we were stark raving mad.

'We look after him for them,' said Patsy. 'We send them photographs and tell them how he's doing.'

There was an embarrassed silence. Mr Munton was obviously not comfortable to be in the home of people who took photographs of a pig to send to people in America.

'So what do you do with your spare time?' Patsy asked him.

'Oh, I'm bit of a party animal,' laughed Mr Munton. 'My fiancée's family are very musical,' he went on. 'Her brother is an actor so we go to a lot of parties and openings and that sort of thing. We know all sorts of really famous and important people.'

'Oh how exciting!' said Patsy. 'What's your fiancée's brother's name?'

'Ludovic Parsons. You might not have heard of him. He avoids cheap publicity and just concentrates on making good connections in the theatrical world.'

Patsy looked at me. We both shook our heads.

'He mainly does stage work,' said Mr Munton. 'He's appeared in several London shows.'

'Ah,' I said, trying to sound respectful.

'Of course he knows quite a few people who've been on television,' he said. 'The girl in that washing powder advert that everyone is talking about will probably be there at this evening's party. And her boyfriend plays the giant duckling in that toilet roll advert that the experts all say is pretty well guaranteed to win all the advertising awards this autumn.'

Patsy and I nodded and tried to look awed.

There was something about Mr Munton which made me feel slightly uncomfortable.

Maybe I was just feeling slightly paranoid, but I got the impression that he was sitting in judgement on me and, indeed, on my patients and their lives. Looking back, I think that the problem was that he was just so damned superior.

'So what brought you to Bilbury?' I asked. 'Do you see yourself working in a rural, single-handed practice one day?'

It didn't seem very likely but I couldn't help wondering why he was in Bilbury for the day.

Mr Munton looked a little startled. 'Oh, good heavens no!' he said. 'I was only here because the Dean said we all had to have some outside experience. I suppose I might go into general practice if all else fails but I was planning on a career as a hospital consultant of some kind.'

'Right,' I said.

'If you manage to combine an NHS career with a decent, private practice you can make quite good money,' said the man whose girlfriend was related to a man who knew a girl whose boyfriend played a duck in a commercial for toilet rolls.

'Yes,' I agreed. 'I believe so.'

I was exhausted by him and was quietly hoping that he would leave as soon as possible.

'Actually, I didn't ask to spend time in a general practice,' said Mr Munton. 'I was rather hoping to be able to spend the day with one of the chaps in Harley Street. But it was all rather arbitrary. They didn't let us choose what we did with our day's practical experience. I think they put our names into a hat and then just allocated us according to chance.'

'Couldn't you say 'No'?' asked Patsy.

'Oh no, it was one of those voluntary experiences that are compulsory.'

'Well, I'm sorry you were disappointed with what you were given,' I said.

'That's OK,' said Mr Munton. 'Not your fault at all.'

'No,' I said. 'I don't think it was.'

'Oh, one thing I meant to ask you, was that a normal surgery?' said Mr Munton, helping himself to another biscuit. This time he took one of the biscuits with cream in the middle. 'I have to write some sort of report. And you seemed to spend a lot of time with old people. Do you think they're worth all that effort?'

I thought for a moment. 'Oh yes, I think it was a fairly normal surgery,' I replied. 'It was shorter than most of my surgeries and in the summer the surgeries are much, much longer, of course.' I really didn't want to respond to his comment about my older patients though I confess it rather alarmed me that a final year medical student should think that way. I was actually rather glad that he didn't want to go into general practice.

He frowned. 'Why are the surgeries longer in the summer?'

'Because we have a lot of visitors in the area; people come in with sunburn, cuts and grazes, insect stings and food poisoning.'

'Insect stings? People come to you after they've been stung by an insect?'

'Of course they do. A horse fly bite can hurt a hell of a lot. And people get rather worried.'

'A horse fly? What's one of those?'

'Large, stoutly built flies which live on blood. Well, I think it's only the female which does the biting. They get their name because they take bites out of horses. But they also rather enjoy munching on people.'

'Oh,' he said, obviously quite bored by this short dissertation. 'I see.' He still seemed puzzled. 'Why would people come to this part of the world for their holidays?'

'Beautiful countryside and coast, lots of walking, wild birds to be seen, beaches and, even in bad weather, the majesty of the sea!' I said. I could see that Patsy was amazed that anyone could not see the attractions of a part of the world where she had been brought up and had spent all her life.

'Oh, I see,' said Mr Munton, who obviously didn't see at all.

'What did you think of the surgery you saw?' asked Patsy.

Inside I winced but I wanted to hear what he had to say.

'It all seemed rather simple,' said Mr Munton. 'I don't think there was anything that a third year medical student couldn't have dealt with.' He paused and thought for a moment. 'I think maybe a good many of the patients could have been dealt with by a nurse. And to be honest, I think the whole thing could have been finished in half the time. I don't think I'd have allowed patients so much time to talk about their problems. You could speed things up quite a lot.'

Patsy and I exchanged glances.

Our rather smug medical student sounded very, very bored. I didn't think I had ever come across anyone quite so self-satisfied. He was not, I thought, the sort of person to suffer unduly with the burden of a conscience or a sense of responsibility. I was, however, slightly surprised that he was not only confidently prepared to teach me my business but also confident that he could do so. And I got the feeling that he thought I should be grateful for his advice.

But the bottom line was that I felt quite sure that Mr Munton had ahead of him a meteoric and unstoppable rise to the very top of the profession; halting only when he had become President of at least one of the Royal Colleges and collected a knighthood or a peerage. And it occurred to me, for the umpteenth time, that worldly success often comes to those who have done nothing to deserve it and who live in blissful ignorance of the world around them and the other people in it.

I didn't remember ever feeling quite so confident when I was a medical student. I wondered whether Mr Munton was unique or a typical example of his generation. I was not, I confess, very much interested in finding out.

'So you've not been convinced that general practice is for you?' I said.

He looked up at the ceiling as though he might find the answer written on the plasterwork. 'No, no, certainly not. I really don't think a country practice would do for me,' he said. 'To be frank, I think I'm perhaps looking for more of a challenge. I have always rather fancied a career in dermatology. Or maybe I might consider psychiatry as a speciality. There was a psychiatrist in London who looked after all the celebrities. He was rumoured to be making a fortune. His name was Eckersley but I gather he disappeared rather suddenly. I don't know what happened to him. I think I'd like a career in some area which allowed me to earn decent money but left me plenty of time to enjoy other activities.'

He made it pretty clear that whatever speciality he chose to grace with his professional presence would be expected to be damned grateful to be chosen.

He slurped some tea and helped himself to another biscuit; a bourbon. I noticed that he was eating all the fancy ones, leaving Patsy and me the plain digestives and the rich tea biscuits.

'If I do agree to go into general practice, I would be looking for a partnership in London somewhere.'

He mentioned Kensington and St John's Wood as being more his cup of tea.

Both are parts of London where the residents all have butlers, maids, chauffeurs and au pair girls. But I didn't think Mr Munton would be prepared to deal with the health problems of the butlers, maids, chauffeurs and au pair girls.

'Must be going,' he said, putting his cup down on top of a small pile of correspondence on my desk. He gave us both a wave and headed for the door. A few moments later, I heard the sound of his sports car firing up. Daddy, I thought, must be quite rich.

I moved the cup off my pile of letters and put it back on the tray.

'He appears to be looking for more of a challenge,' said Patsy. 'I'm afraid he obviously found your morning surgery rather dull and undemanding.'

I looked at her.

'Are you going to have to entertain any more of these young almost-doctors?'

'No.' I looked at my watch. 'My teaching days started two and half hours ago and finished a minute ago.'

I was actually rather depressed. I had been patronised by a very supercilious young man and I felt vaguely dissatisfied with my professional self. It had not been an exciting surgery. I hadn't saved any lives but as far as I was aware I hadn't killed anyone either. On balance, I thought I had probably made a couple of people's lives a little easier, which is often all a country doctor can hope to do.

'Oh goody,' said Patsy.

'He ate all the best biscuits.'

'I know. He ate three jammy dodgers. There were only three in the box.'

'What are jammy dodgers?' I asked.

'The round biscuits with the jam in the middle.'

'Oh, I like those.'

'Me too. Did you know that they're named after that character Roger the Dodger in *The Beano* comic?'

'I didn't know that,' I said. 'If I'd strangled Mr Munton I could have buried him in the garden. We could have said he'd left as planned but had talked about driving up to Scotland to shoot some grouse. I don't think the world would have missed him very much.'

'Are you allowed to strangle snooty medical students?'

'Oh I think so. As long as you don't strangle more than two a year.'

Patsy sighed. 'Too late now. He's gone. Another missed opportunity.'

Just then the telephone went.

I listened for a while, made a few noises of appreciation, said 'thank you' and 'thank you very much' and then put the telephone receiver back on its rest.

'Do you have to go out?' asked Patsy.

'No. That was Mr Longwoody's daughter. She lives in Scotland and she'd been down here a couple of days ago just to see how her father was doing. She apologised for having to rush back without seeing me but just rang to say thank you to me for looking after her father. She wanted to tell me that she was pleased to know that he was in such good hands.'

Patsy gave me a hug.

The telephone call from Mr Longwoody's daughter could not have come at a more opportune moment for it banished the strange feeling of discontent and professional dissatisfaction which had lingered after Mr Munton's departure.

We all need a little reassurance from time to time.

The Detective

The summer was in full swing when my friend William brought his family down to Bilbury for the weekend.

William is a GP who works in a large, modern practice near to the town of Wolverhampton, right in the heart of the English Midlands. He is probably the brightest person I have ever met. When we talk he always seemed to be giving me his full attention, but I could never quite dismiss from my mind the thought that he only needed to use one part of his brain to concentrate fully on our conversation. I was always conscious that while talking to me his brain was dealing with half a dozen other issues at the same time, and that he was giving them his full attention too, in the way that Grand Masters such as Bobby Fischer could play two dozen games of chess simultaneously and, if asked to do so, play them all blindfolded.

When William got married I was his best man. His wife, Brenda, was Patsy's best friend outside Bilbury. I think the friendship helped them both a great deal; since they were both married to family doctors they had some understanding of the strange and sometimes demanding world in which we live.

The fact is, however, that although William and I were both GPs, and theoretically did the same jobs, we lived completely different lives and practised in very different ways.

William worked with a number of other doctors and a vast support staff. Most of his patients lived in neatly labelled houses or in blocks of flats. The streets where he worked were well lit and everywhere he went the roads were wide enough for cars to travel in two different directions at once. William had 2,500 patients on his personal list, and he and his partners and their medical assistants looked after a huge practice of 15,000 patients. The practice was so big that it even employed its own accountant and the accountant had an assistant!

I worked by myself with Patsy and Miss Johnson helping to answer the telephone, organise the pharmacy and generally do everything that in William's practice was done by a team of receptionists and ancillaries. I had only around 600 patients (all of whom I knew by name) and they lived in around 250 houses and cottages scattered around a fairly large area of countryside. None of the homes I visited had numbers and some did not even have names. The roads on which I drove were hardly ever wide enough to allow traffic to travel in two directions at once and without passing places and gateways it would have been impossible for anyone to go anywhere. When I went out in the car, I spent almost as much time in reverse gear as in a forward gear.

Our practices were, in every imaginable way, quite different.

But in the end our work was, of course, exactly the same.

In William's surgery, a patient would enter his consulting room, sit down and present a history of his symptoms, signs and worries.

And in my surgery in Bilbury, a patient would enter my consulting room, sit down and present a history of his or her symptoms, signs and worries.

No difference.

The day was still warm and William and I were sitting in the summerhouse, enjoying the remains of another wonderful day. Patsy and Brenda were in the house getting the children ready for bed. William's son, Peter, was old enough to believe that he should be allowed to stay up with the grown-ups so William and Brenda let him stay up for an extra half an hour. Fortunately, Bilbury Grange, a rambling old house, had enough bedrooms for William's two children to have one each.

William and Brenda come to see us as often as they could and they were always welcome. Benjamin Franklin, writing in his *Poor Richard's Almanack*, wrote that 'fish and visitors both stink after three days' and as far as many visitors are concerned he was undoubtedly right. But William and Brenda, and their children, never 'stank', never annoyed and never outstayed their welcome.

I had taken a bag of sunflower hearts out with me and I put a couple of handfuls on the ground just outside the summer house. William and I watched as a tame pheasant wandered up the garden, headed straight for the sunflower hearts and proceeded to take his fill. When he'd finished, he wiped his beak carefully on the grass, first this way and then that way, and then headed for the stone bird bath which I kept filled with water throughout the year. When he'd drunk to his satisfaction, he hopped down off the bird bath and again wiped his beak on the grass. He always wiped it half a dozen times.

As the pheasant wandered away, one of our tame squirrels arrived outside the summer house. He finished off most of the remaining sunflower hearts and then he too wandered off to the bird bath. He leapt up and took a long drink. Experts on squirrel behaviour sometimes claim that squirrels never drink water. Well ours did. Maybe the squirrels hadn't bothered to read the textbooks.

Finally, a robin appeared and finished off the few remaining sunflower hearts before he too flew to the bird bath for a drink.

'Does that happen every evening?' asked Will, who had been watching this display in quiet astonishment.

'Most evenings,' I said. 'Sometimes there are two or three squirrels and a couple of blackbirds.'

We sat in silence for a while longer; looking out at nothing in particular. A few rabbits appeared at the far end of the lawn. They chased each other around and ate a good deal of grass and some daisies.

'I had a medical student here for a day last month,' I said.

'From Birmingham University?'

'Yes.'

Will and I both attended the same medical school at the same time. That was how we met.

'They managed to persuade you to take one, did they?'

'Only because they were clever enough to give me several months' notice. I said 'yes' because the date they suggested seemed to be a long way away.'

'They're crafty like that,' said Will.

'Did you have one?'

'Oh no! Good heavens no! We had one last year.'

'Didn't go well?'

'Absolutely bloody disaster! They sent us some girl of about fourteen. Well, she looked fourteen. She knew everything. She was so full of herself that there wasn't any room for anything else.'

'Maybe we're getting old,' I said.

'We are. But it wasn't just that. They seem to be giving them 'confidence pills' these days.'

'I'm afraid I won't be having another student.'

We sat in silence again and watched the midges doing what midges do in the early evening.

'Do you mind?' asked Will, taking his pipe out of his jacket pocket and holding it up for approval. The request was a courtesy. He knew that I would never say 'No'. When he is at home he smokes only in the garden shed, in the greenhouse or on the patio.

'Of course not,' I said. 'Is Brenda still nagging you to give it up?'

'Brenda and everyone at the surgery,' confessed William with a sheepish grin. 'Even Peter has a go at me now.'

I watched as he took out the paraphernalia which smokers always carry with them. The tobacco pouch, the box of smokers' matches, the little silver gadget used for pressing down the tobacco and cleaning out the bowl – all came out of his pockets and were placed carefully on the wooden table in front of him. It's the one thing I always envy pipe smokers. 'That's a new pouch, isn't it?' I asked, nodding towards the tobacco pouch he was using.

'Brenda bought it for my birthday,' said Will. 'The old one had a hole in it and was looking a bit ropey.'

'But Brenda doesn't approve of you smoking!'

'No, she doesn't. But she knows that an occasional pipe full of tobacco helps me to relax.' He paused, opened the pouch and took out some tobacco. 'Did I tell you that Jerry had another heart attack? It was quite a severe one this time.'

I said he hadn't and that I was sorry to hear it.

I had never met Jerry but Will had talked about him. He was one of the partners in William's practice. 'How old is he?'

'Forty six. He doesn't smoke but he drinks too much beer and he's hugely overweight. He has always rather reminded me of a character out of a novel by P.G.Wodehouse. It is difficult to say 'Tchah!' without sounding like a bad actor playing the villain in a Victorian melodrama but Jerry manages it perfectly. I think it is his favourite saying. And he is the only person I've ever heard using the word Egad!'

'Forty six is young. That's too young; far too young.'

Whatever your age it is always rather alarming to hear of people in their 40s becoming seriously ill.

'It certainly is,' agreed William. 'That's his third heart attack in two years. They've scheduled him for heart surgery and he's going to retire. We're looking for a replacement partner.' He packed some of the tobacco into the bowl of his pipe, pressing it down first with his thumb and then with his little silver gadget. 'I don't suppose you'd be interested?'

'No thank you,' I said immediately. 'But thank you for asking.'

'I told the others I would ask you first. They all agreed. We're making quite good money now. We have quite a bit of insurance work and we look after the staff in a couple of large, local factories so we get extra money for that. And you'd only be on call for one or two nights a week – instead of the seven nights a week you're on call now.'

'I'm flattered by the offer.'

'Talk it over with Patsy before you give me a definite 'No'. Brenda would love it if you two moved up into our area. There are some lovely houses on the market. You won't find anything as big as this place, of course. And you don't get such big gardens in the town. But you could get somewhere pretty nice near to us. One of the biggest estate agents is a patient of mine and we play golf most Sundays. He'd be happy to help you find something suitable.'

I said I would talk to Patsy. I knew what she would say but I said I would tell her about the offer all the same.

We sat in pleasant silence for a while. You can do that with old friends. I sometimes think that silence is the true sign of friendship. Will puffed at his pipe and I enjoyed the aroma second hand. The smoke kept the midges away, for which I was very grateful. All insects seem to regard my body as a fast food restaurant. The smoke from William's pipe even kept the horse-flies away.

'We had a break-in at the surgery two weeks ago,' said Will suddenly and apropos of absolutely nothing. I like conversations which veer from one topic to another without any warning. Most of the conversations which I had with William were like that.

'Drugs?'

'Yes, someone broke into the main part of the building, by-passed the alarm and stole our stock of morphine.'

'Did they just steal the morphine?'

'No, that was the odd thing. When the police came, it was the dangerous drug cupboard that we checked first, of course. But then our senior pharmacist checked the rest of the stock and discovered that some other stuff was missing too. The petty cash hadn't been touched but there were some other pills missing.'

'Your senior pharmacist! How many pharmacists do you have?'

'Two and a trainee.'

'Good heavens!'

'We have a special manager to look after the staff now. She's called a Personnel Manager. She organises the rotas and holidays, supervises wages, bonuses and so on. She even handles the recruitment process when we need new receptionists, cleaners and so on. She's very good. She used to work for one of the big car companies. She wants us to buy one of these new office sized computers and keep all our staff records in it. She says we ought to be able to keep the accounts on the computer too. My partners are a bit sceptical but I think I'll be able to talk them round. Mrs Bird, that's the new personnel manager, reckons that one day doctors will keep their patients' records on computers.'

'But not yet, surely?'

I must have sounded terrified for William laughed. 'No, I don't think we'll be doing that for a few years. But it would certainly be good to keep the accounts on a computer. They make special software now that deals with all the financial stuff.'

'Crumbs.'

'Is Miss Johnson still your entire staff?'

'Yes. And she only works part time. She keeps my accounts in a little black notebook. She buys a new one each year from F.W.Woolworth in Barnstaple and she keeps the old ones on a shelf in the cupboard under the stairs. Did the police catch your thief?'

'They did. And I'm proud to say that I had a Sherlock Holmes moment which contributed to them catching him.'

'Tell me more!'

'In addition to clearing out all our morphine, the thief also took 200 diuretic tablets, 200 digitalis tablets, 400 blood pressure tablets and four bottles of a non-steroidal anti-inflammatory for arthritis.'

'Aha!'

'Exactly! You've guessed. It seemed a reasonable supposition that the thief might be a patient of ours who was taking pills. I talked to my partners and the reception staff and we decided we only had half a dozen patients who took that combination of pills.'

'And five of them were little old ladies who were wheelchair bound?'

William laughed. 'Not a bad guess. We managed to name them and it turned out that five of them were old aged pensioners who seemed unlikely to have been able to squeeze through a small window, let alone disable a fairly sophisticated alarm.'

'And the sixth?'

'The sixth was a bloke in his mid-40s who had heart disease and arthritis and was taking all the pills which were stolen. We knew he had a rather dodgy history. He'd been inside for drug dealing and he had a bit of a history of breaking and entering. He tries to look respectable but, sadly, he somehow manages to look like 90% of all police photo-fit pictures and he is without a doubt the sort of fellow the police are always 'anxious to interview in connection with their enquiries'.'

'You keep all that sort of information in your files?'

'No, no! We're not that efficient. But one of our receptionists lives in the same street as this chap. She was the one who spotted his name on the list of possible suspects.'

'Together with the five pensioners?'

'Exactly. Our suspicions were confirmed when we looked for his medical records. The idiot had taken his records out of one of the filing cabinets, presumably to check on the names of the drugs he was taking, and then he'd just left his notes on the counter in the pharmacy. None of us would ever do that. The practice manager is very strict about making sure that all the records go back into the proper filing cabinet when they're finished with.'

'So what did you do?'

'It was a bit tricky, really. We had a meeting but couldn't decide whether it was ethical to give his name to the police as a suspect. We rang the lawyers at the Medical Defence Union and we asked someone at the British Medical Association and everyone we spoke to said it would be a bit dodgy to give his name because we'd only identified him by looking at his medical records. One of my partners thought we could perhaps just sort of suggest the idea of the burglary being done by a patient to the police and let them get a warrant to check our records but none of us liked that idea. It seemed totally unethical.'

'So, what the devil did you do?'

'I went round to his home that evening, banged on his door and told him we wanted our drugs back or else we'd tell the police.'

'You did what?' I was astonished.

'What else could we do? We couldn't let him get away with it. And we certainly didn't want all that morphine on the local market. We have a big enough drug addiction problem as it is. We don't carry all that much morphine in stock but these drug dealers cut the stuff and turn a few dozen doses into a few hundred doses.'

'What did the chap say?'

'He was a bit threatening at first but I told him that everyone at the practice knew I was calling on him and that if anything happened to me the police would be called.'

'Did he admit taking the stuff?'

'Oh, he mumbled about being at a football match but I just stared at him and waited and eventually he confessed.'

'Did you get it all back?'

'Everything. Every last phial and tablet. And I told him he had to pay for the broken window and the call out fee to the alarm people. I even got him to recommend a better alarm system.'

'And the police?'

'We told them that the thief had returned everything. We said he must have felt guilty. The police were happy enough to be able to put it down as a solved case.'

I congratulated Will and told him I thought he was a braver man than I would have been.

'Oh, I wasn't worried too much,' he said. 'The fellow is just a lobcock. He has no myrmidons and I guessed he'd turn out to be a mugwump.'

I laughed out loud.

William, who was also laughing, then admitted that before coming down to Bilbury he had spent some time finding odd, old-fashioned names for individuals with slightly dodgy habits.

'I know a myrmidon is an obedient follower, but what the devil is a lobcock and who on earth is a mugwump?' I asked him.

'A lobcock is someone who is a blundering fool, someone a bit stupid, and a mugwump is someone who backs down when they're under pressure.'

I liked William's new words so much that I dug out a notebook and together we began to create a new list of slightly archaic words which we thought deserved to be revived.

After that, we sat for another half an hour in the summerhouse talking about everything and nothing, as friends will when they have a little time and haven't seen each other for a while.

When it became chilly we went indoors.

I lit a log fire and I insisted on William telling Patsy the story of his Sherlock Holmes moment.

Patsy was as impressed as I had been. And rather startled at William's courage in going round to the fellow's house to confront him.

I then dug out all the dictionaries I could find and William and I went through them searching for more odd words to put into our latest list. (The resultant list is at the back of this book.)

That evening, as we got ready for bed, I told Patsy about William's offer of a partnership in his practice in the Midlands.

'Do you want to accept it?' she asked.

I looked at her and raised an eyebrow but didn't say anything.

'Thank heavens,' Patsy said. She paused and thought about it for a moment. 'But it was very kind of him to ask.'

'He asked me to mention it to you and I said I would.'

'Will he be upset at your turning him down?'

'No, I don't think he seriously expected us to take the offer. He's asked before and always had the same answer.'

'Point out that if we moved up to the Midlands, he and Brenda wouldn't be able to come down to Bilbury for the weekend,' said Patsy.

'Good idea,' I said. 'If he'd thought about that he probably wouldn't have offered me the job in the first place!'

The Carpenter

Mr Horace Berry walked into the consulting room like a man with too many legs and sat down with a thump which I feared would break the chair. He was massively overweight and he managed to look miserable and bad tempered at the same time.

Mr Berry was a descendant of the famous hangman, James Berry. He told me this, apropos of absolutely nothing, but with obvious pride, within minutes of our first meeting. He told me that James Berry had achieved unwanted notoriety in the 19th century for attempting three times to hang James Lee, the Babbacombe murderer, and failing every time. The fiasco had taken place at Exeter prison and after the third attempt had proved unsuccessful, the hanging had been cancelled and Mr Lee's sentence had been commuted to life imprisonment. (In view of the connection with my patient, there is a brief account of the attempted hanging, why it failed and the prisoner's subsequent life, in one of the appendices at the back of this book.)

In addition to having such a distinguished ancestor, Mr Berry was a combative sort of person; the sort of fellow who, if he saw a fight (whether physical or verbal) would probably not be able to resist the temptation to get involved.

And he believed, quite firmly, that all his health problems were as a result of his having given up work.

'I was perfectly healthy until I was forced to stop working,' he complained baldly and quite bitterly.

Puzzled, I looked at him. Retirement can sometimes cause depression and a sense of worthlessness but I hadn't heard of it causing physical health problems.

'I was as fit as a fiddle when I working,' continued Mr Berry defiantly. 'It was having to give up work that made me ill.'

He spoke with great certainty, as though he had been given official confirmation, in triplicate, of his suspicion.

His wife, who was sitting next to him, nodded slightly, as if in confirmation.

I knew Mrs Berry, his wife, quite well. She had been to see me several times because she suffered from chronic blepharitis, a condition affecting her eyelids. The tiny oil glands at the base of the eyelashes become clogged and the result can be irritation and red eyes. To make matters worse, Mrs Berry often developed small but annoying infections which affected her eyelids.

After I had shown Mrs Berry how to use cotton buds to clean the edges of her eyelids, she usually managed to deal with these problems herself but occasionally she needed help. On the day about which I write, however, she was in my surgery in a supporting role.

'So, what can I do for you?' I asked him.

'I get pains in my knees and my hips and in my back too. I want you to do something about that. You need to give me something to take. And I get tired and out of breath if I do much walking.'

'When did you retire?'

He answered instantly. 'I stopped work in the autumn of 1963,' he said. 'My last day of work was Friday 25th of October.'

His wife nodded her agreement. 'Friday the 25th,' she confirmed.

'Is it not possible that the health problems you've acquired might simply be a result of your getting older?' I asked, hoping that the enquiry sounded moderately tactful.

'Oh no,' he said quite definitely.

'Have you put on weight since you retired?'

'Of course I have! I wasn't always this fat. When I was working I was busy all the time.'

'Do you eat more now than you did when you were working?'

'A little, I suppose.' He shrugged, defiantly, defensively. 'There's nothing much else to do, is there?'

I suspected that Mr Berry had always been a well-built man. But I guessed that during the years of his retirement he had gradually grown beyond well-built, gone at quite a pace through overweight, raced through outsized and finally, settled comfortably into obese.

'When I was working I was fine. I had no aches or pains. I could run a mile and climb a tree,' insisted Mr Berry. He sighed. It was a long, sad sigh that ended with a whistling wheeze. I rather doubted the claims he had made about his ability to run a mile and climb a

165

tree. I suspected that it had probably been quite a few decades since he'd been able to run anywhere or climb anything more than a stepladder. 'Now I have a job to get up and down the stairs,' he complained. He turned to his wife for support. 'Isn't that so mother?'

Mrs Berry, who looked as though her mind was somewhere else, nodded her agreement.

I wondered how she felt about being called 'mother' since they had no children.

'Mind you, I'm not complaining,' said Mr Berry who seemed to me to be doing exactly that. He moved his bulk on the chair and the chair's legs creaked in distress. In horse racing terms they were carrying top weight. 'I've had a good life and the missus and I have had a long and happy life together.' He turned to his wife and patted her on the knee.

'A long and happy life together,' repeated Mrs Berry. She then thought for a moment before looking at him and then at me. 'Happy for him and long for me.'

Having delivered this unexpected bon mot, she cackled, sounding remarkably like one of Macbeth's not so jolly witches sitting round the cooking pot and enjoying the warmth of their camp fire.

Mr Berry who looked as though he'd left his sense of humour somewhere but couldn't remember where he'd put it, looked at her sternly.

'What did you do for a living?' I asked him, thinking it was time to change the subject a little.

'What was my job?'

'Yes. What was your job?'

'I was a carpenter. I was a very good carpenter wasn't I, mother?' He even managed to sound combative when making a bald statement such as this.

His wife nodded.

'Where did you work?'

'I worked for a kitchen fitting company. We did bespoke kitchens. We used all the best materials and made beautiful kitchen furniture: cupboards, worktops and so on. I even used to make free standing tables that were designed to match the work surfaces and to fit into available spaces.'

I could hear the pride in his voice and I thought that I was, for the first time, beginning to understand him a little. I have always believed that it is often impossible for a general practitioner to treat his patients well unless he understands a little about their lives, their hopes and their fears.

'What happened?'

'What do you mean, 'what happened?'?'

'Why did you lose your job?'

'Oh. The company I worked for went bust. We were destroyed by these companies which sell ready-made kitchens. They sell rubbish. All their stuff is made out of plastic and hardboard and plywood. Unskilled workmen just glue it all together. Superficially it looks good and it's a lot cheaper than hand-made furniture built out of real wood so they sell a lot of it. We couldn't compete so we went bust and I lost my job. They should line up all those bastards and shoot them.'

'And you haven't worked since?' I asked. I assumed that the bastards he wanted shooting were the men putting together the cheap kitchen furniture.

'There's no work in North Devon for a carpenter,' said Mr Berry. 'I applied for a job at one of the shipyards but they weren't hiring skilled men. They just had openings for apprentices. I tried for a place at one of the local builders but they weren't hiring either. They don't have enough work. These days, people prefer to buy that Swedish rubbish you put together yourself. It's a hell of a lot cheaper than proper stuff.'

'So you haven't worked since 1963?'

'No.'

I looked at Mr Berry's medical records. 'And you're 61 now?'

'Yes.'

He looked a lot older than 61. If I'd had to guess I'd have put him at nearer 70-years-old. I told him to undress so that I could check him over.

Apart from the excess weight, there wasn't much wrong with him. To my surprise, his blood pressure was fairly normal. The systolic pressure reading was a little high but the diastolic was fine. His heart was beating fine and I could not hear any abnormalities. It seemed to me that all his problems were caused by his weight. It was all that excess weight that was putting a strain on his back and his hips. It was all that excess weight that made it difficult for him to move about. The excess weight made it difficult for him to breathe and he even had nasty patches of eczema in the skin folds caused by his excess weight.

'Have you tried to lose weight?' I asked him. 'You'd feel a lot better and be able to move about much easier if you lost a couple of stones.'

I was tempted to explain to him that knee and hip joints are designed to carry the weight of one body, not two but I thought he might explode if I did so. He seemed to be a man who was permanently angry. The fact that he could still remember the exact date when he'd finished work suggested that he was still brooding about it.

'That's easy for you to say!' snapped Mr Berry.

'I put him on a diet I found in one of my magazines,' said Mrs Berry. 'You eat nothing but fruit and vegetables on three days of the week, nothing but protein on Wednesdays and nothing but carbohydrates on the other days.'

I stared at her in disbelief.

'That's the diet?'

'Oh yes. They say that people lose huge amounts of weight on it. You can choose which days you eat the fruit and vegetables and which days you eat the carbohydrates.'

I turned to Mr Berry. 'How long have you been on this diet?'

'Six weeks.'

'And have you lost any weight?'

'I've lost a pound,' said Mr Berry. He said this proudly, and clearly expected a round of applause though I guessed he would probably make do with a word of praise.

'Congratulations!' I said, trying not to sound in the slightest bit sarcastic.

It occurred to me that at the rate he was going it would be at least another four or five years before he managed to get his weight down to an acceptable level. Looking at him I wondered if he was going to live long enough to lose the weight he needed to lose.

'What hobbies do you have?' I asked him, still trying to find out more about him and his life.

'I don't have time for hobbies,' he said. 'Never have. I've always worked hard and just wanted to sit down in the evenings and at weekends.'

'He's always read the newspaper and watched the television in the evenings,' said Mrs Berry.

'I've not been one of those who spends his time in the pub,' said Mr Berry. 'I prefer to stay at home, with the wife, and save my money.'

'We have a job making ends meet these days,' added Mrs Berry. 'I make a little extra by doing a little book-keeping for one or two people. I help Gilly with her accounts.'

'Gilly Parsons at the Duck and Puddle?' I enquired. Gilly and her husband Frank are the joint landlords of the village pub.

'Yes,' nodded Mrs Berry.

'You don't do any gardening?' I said to Mr Berry. Many retired men in the village are proud of their gardens. I know quite a few who grow most of their own vegetables and produce more than their families can eat.

'Never been keen on it,' said Mr Berry. 'Mother looks after the garden. Cuts the grass and so on. I'd do it if I could but my hips won't let me.'

'I think you need a better, more effective diet,' I told him. 'You need to lose more than a pound a month.'

Mr Berry looked at me rather fiercely. 'How much more?'

'I think you ought to be able to lose two pounds a week. That would mean you would be losing half a stone in a month. And in six months you'd be much fitter and healthier.'

'Half a stone a month!'

'Absolutely!' I said.

But I really didn't think that just losing weight was going to be enough to make Mr Berry feel more content and I rather suspected that just being fitter and healthier weren't going to be enough to give him the incentive he needed. He needed something else to aim for. He needed a purpose. We all need a purpose in our lives and since he had lost his job, Mr Berry's life had been pretty well without any purpose. He'd just been marking time and there was no real meaning to his life.

'We'll try your diet,' said Mrs Berry firmly.

I took one of my diet booklets out of a drawer in my desk and handed it to her. When I first took over the practise, I knew that I would be faced with quite a few patients who needed to lose weight. I therefore prepared a booklet containing advice on losing weight

169

and had a thousand printed at a shop in Barnstaple. Since I'd been in practice, I had distributed a fifth of them – with quite a number of those going to visitors and holidaymakers. Patsy thought that I'd perhaps printed rather too many and I agreed with her that I had, perhaps, been rather ambitious when ordering a thousand copies for a practice that had only 600 patients.

'Have you thought about doing a little carpentry again?' I asked Mr Berry.

'I told you – there are no jobs,' he snapped. 'If there had been any jobs going I'd have applied.' I got the feeling that if we had been sitting in a pub he would have stood up and invited me outside.

'I realise that there aren't any jobs,' I said. 'I wasn't suggesting that you try working for someone else. I meant working for yourself.'

Puzzled, he looked at me. It was obviously something he had never considered. 'My working days are over,' he said, as though he were 98-years-old and had already been measured for his coffin. This was clearly something he had told himself and come to believe.

Robert Browning encouraged us to believe that 'the best is yet to be' but there is a certain breed of Englishmen (and women) who sometimes feel more comfortable assuming that the worst, not the best, is yet to come. It is, I suppose, easier to deal with the inevitable exigencies and disappointments encountered in life when you are not expecting too much.

'Do you still have your tools?' I asked him. I was pretty sure of the answer since I knew that most skilled workmen had their own tools and guarded them rather jealously.

'Of course I do. They're in a box in the shed. I haven't touched them for years. But I wrapped them in oiled cloths.'

'And do you have somewhere that you could work?'

'We have the shed,' said Mrs Berry. 'It's got a workbench.'

'It's full of junk,' said Mr Berry. 'There's no room to move.'

'We could easily clear it out,' said his wife. 'It's mostly filled with rubbish. We could have a big bonfire.'

'But who am I going to get to tell me what to make? And who will pay me?' demanded Mr Berry.

'There's always a demand for decent furniture,' I told him. 'A lot of people buy old furniture because it's better made than the new stuff. If they knew a carpenter who could make decent tables, wardrobes and beds then they might commission him to make exactly what they wanted.'

'People buy antiques,' said Mr Berry. 'But that's all they're interested in.'

'I don't agree with you!' I said. 'Lots of people prefer to buy old furniture that was made back in Victorian and Edwardian days and most of that stuff isn't classified as antique but it's better made than the new flat pack stuff that seems to be so fashionable.' I waved a hand around my surgery. 'There's nothing in here that's antique but it's old and it's all good, solid furniture.' I rapped my knuckles on my desk. 'This is a good solid desk but it certainly isn't an antique.'

'There you are, you see!' said Mr Berry. 'Proper wooden furniture lasts for years. That new stuff that people build themselves won't last ten years.'

'No, it probably won't,' I agreed.

'But how would we find people who wanted to have new furniture made for them?' asked Mrs Berry.

'Advertise!' I said. 'Peter Marshall has a noticeboard at his shop. You could pin up a card there. And you could advertise in the Parish Newsletter. It costs hardly anything to advertise there and you'd be reaching the very people you need to reach.'

Mr Berry looked uncertain. 'You mean I should start my own business?'

'Exactly!'

'I'm a bit old for that, aren't I?'

'Don't be daft!' I said. 'I bet there are a lot of people in North Devon who would jump at the chance to have some bespoke furniture made. You could make tables and cupboards to fit those odd little corners that most old houses seem to have.'

'The doctor is right,' said Mrs Berry. 'Having something to do would do you a power of good. You'd be doing something you enjoy. You've always said that you miss your work. This is a chance to get your tools out and make some more good furniture.'

Mr Berry looked brighter for a moment and then his face clouded. 'I could never run my own business,' he said. 'It would mean keeping books and accounts and doing taxes and that sort of thing. That sort of stuff was never my strong point.'

'You've got the answer sitting next to you!' I pointed out. 'Your wife is a bookkeeper. I'm sure she'd be happy to handle the finances for you.'

'Of course I would!' said Mrs Berry. 'I'd love to. We would be running our own little business and doing it together.'

Mr Berry did not look convinced.

I have found that on the whole, the elderly tend to be less enthusiastic about taking risks than the young. The young are reckless risk takers because the only thing they know for sure is that they are immortal. Older folk are far more conscious of death and their own mortality than the young. They are cautious because they know that death is hanging around, leaning on the next lamppost, waiting for them, scythe at the ready, and they are anxious to cheat the inevitable for as long as possible. They prefer to keep their heads down and to leave plenty of room in their lives for the problems and the emergencies which they know are an inevitable part of life. Older folk worry more because they are aware how easily things can go wrong and just how much life likes to bowl a googly right at the moment when you're expecting a straight ball.

Eventually, when he left the surgery, Mr Berry had agreed that he and his wife would write out a few advertisements and see what happened. And he had agreed to give up the magazine diet that wasn't working and to try my diet sheet.

Within six months, Mr Berry had lost three stones and he was looking like a different man. He was no longer complaining about his hips or his knees and he had far less difficulty in getting about.

I saw Mr Berry driving his new (but second hand) truck a year or so later. There was a brand new oak wardrobe in the back of the truck. I was just coming out of a cottage down near Softly's Bottom and I waved him down.

'How's business?' I asked him.

'Fantastic!' he replied, winding down his window. 'I can't keep up with the orders. I've got a pair of bedside tables and a television cabinet to make before the end of the month. I'm even getting work from outside the village. Last week we had a phone call from someone in Exeter who wants me to make a kitchen table for them.' He grinned and patted his now much flatter stomach. 'Being back at work has made me healthier too!' He obviously still believed that it was working that kept him fit. In a way he was right, of course.

'I'm glad things are going well!' I said.

'Brilliant, absolutely brilliant!' said Mr Berry. 'I'm so glad I had that idea to start out on my own. I often tell mother that it was the best idea I've ever had and the best thing I've ever done – apart from marrying her, of course.'

I told him I was very pleased to hear his good news.

'I've rather proved my point, don't you think, doctor?'

'What point was that?' I asked, rather puzzled.

'I said I was ill because I'd lost my job,' said Mr Berry. 'I don't think you believed me, did you?'

'Well…' I began.

'You can't argue with the facts! I'm working again and now I'm as fit as a fiddle,' he said, proud of himself. 'When I was working I was well. When I stopped working I was ill. Now I'm working and I'm well again. Proof of the pudding, eh? Isn't that what they say?'

'Proof of the pudding!' I agreed, with a nod.

He grinned, winked and put the truck into gear all at the same time. 'Must go – I've got to get this delivered before lunch.'

And with a slight crashing of the gears he was off.

Carlton and Hermione Thorley

'Oh, and there was a call asking you to visit Mr Thorley at home,' said Miss Johnson, when she'd finished giving me the list of my morning calls. 'It's not urgent but they'd like you to call in sometime.'

'Thorley?' I said, puzzled. 'I don't think I know anyone called Thorley. Is he a patient of ours?'

'He's not on our records so he isn't registered as a patient. But I believe they've been living in the village for nearly three years now. Mrs Thorley very occasionally helps with flower arranging at St Dymphnas.'

'And they're definitely living in Bilbury?'

'Yes, I believe so.'

'They moved here three years ago?'

'I think it was about that long ago.'

I frowned. 'I don't remember hearing of anyone called Thorley.'

'I believe they're very shy,' said Miss Johnson. 'They tend to keep themselves to themselves. I've not seen them out and about in the village. I've not seen them at all – apart from Mrs Thorley helping with the flowers from time to time.'

'Whereabouts do they live?'

'Buttercup Cottage.'

'Is that the little pink cottage on the road to Barnstaple?'

'That's the one. It's set back from the road a little way and a lot of people go past without noticing that it's there. It used to be painted yellow. I think the people who lived there before the Thorleys were fond of yellow. And because they'd painted it yellow they called it Buttercup Cottage.'

'And now it's pink?'

Miss Johnson nodded.

'And the Thorleys are not just there on holiday?'

'Oh no, I think they live here in the village. Peter Marshall says that Mrs Thorley pops into his shop quite regularly. Peter says she buys a lot of mincemeat.'

'Mincemeat?'

'She buys it every week apparently. At this time of the year, Peter gets it in just for her. And Peter says she also buys a lot of icing sugar and parsnips.'

When you live in a small village there isn't much that the other villagers don't know. And Miss Johnson is a news gatherer par excellence. If I were ever to run a local paper I would hire her to write the gossip column. 'And so they've definitely moved into the village?'

'I would think so.'

'Right.' I sighed. 'Well, maybe they just like a lot of roast parsnips and have mincemeat instead of marmalade on their morning toast.'

Miss Johnson gave me that look she gives me when she thinks I'm being silly. Miss Johnson isn't entirely sure that she approves of frivolity but she's far too polite to say anything.

To be honest, I was slightly surprised by her news about the Thorleys.

Most people who move into the village like to register with their local general practitioner within a month or so at the most. It was definitely unusual for people to move into the village and live there for three years without popping in to sign up with their GP.

'OK. I'll call in and see what they want.'

And so three quarters of an hour later I drove up to Buttercup Cottage (in all its glorious pinkness) and realised that there was absolutely nowhere to leave the car. The 1930 Rolls Royce 20/25 which I inherited from my predecessor, Dr Brownlow, does eight miles to the gallon when it wants to and rather less when it doesn't, and, as my friend Patchy Fogg once said, it is a car which was definitely built for travelling rather than arriving. It is an absurdly impractical vehicle for a country doctor and it was certainly not built for parking anywhere other than, possibly, on an aircraft runway. I purred along the lane and eventually found an unused gateway where I managed to squeeze the car onto the verge.

After I'd got out of the car I leant, for a few moments, on the five barred gate. The one thing I really like about five barred gates is that, whatever their size and however they are hung, they always seem to be a perfect height for leaning on. I watched the sheep playing in the field and I recognised the paint marks some of them bore – they belonged to Patsy's father, Mr Kennet. I hadn't realised the field was his. Mr Kennet owns a good deal of Bilbury.

As I watched the sheep peacefully grazing and occasionally playing 'hide and seek' and 'king of the castle', it occurred to me that animals never start wars. You never hear of a dozen sheep starting a revolution, breaking away from the flock and announcing that they are taking over the left hand side of the field because it has the lushest grass, do you?

Overhead, jackdaws were swooping and playing in the sky and in the middle distance I could see a raven perched on a fence post. Unlike other members of the crow family, ravens never seem to make much of a fuss about anything. And a dozen seagulls had found something to interest them on the far edge of the field. Seagulls are a part of seaside life, along with the sound of the surf breaking on the shore, the feel of bare feet on warm sand (and even the pain of bare feet on shingle or a rocky beach) and although they make a good deal of mess, and there are those who would like to eradicate them completely, I firmly believe that we would miss them if they were somehow banished.

Like many other Bilbury residents, I like to stand and stare when I have a moment to spare. I couldn't help thinking that when I was a small boy, in the years immediately after World War II, life was extraordinarily simple. It seemed simple then, and in retrospect it is clear that, compared to life today, it was astonishingly simple. In those now distant days, happiness meant a patch of grass, a few hours sunshine, a bottle of dandelion and burdock, a bar of chocolate and a library book.

In the 1950s television broadcasting hours were strictly limited, the telephone was for emergencies and most games involved boards, counters and dice. There was no social media and group activities were limited to conkers in the autumn, slides and snowball fights in the winter, marbles in the spring and swimming and cricket in the summer. The total financial cost of all these activities was insignificant. Electricity was something that gave us lights and very little else, and the absence of central heating meant that on cold, winter days the inside of my bedroom window was covered with magical Jack Frost patterns.

Back when I was a boy, I always enjoyed being outside; riding a bicycle, climbing trees and watching animals. These activities involved a good deal of falling over. Between the ages of 6 and 14 there was barely a day that went by that I didn't have a scab on one or both knees and one or both elbows. Modern children don't do anything to collect scabs, let alone have time to pick at them. It is a matter of record that as a boy I always had at least one scab worth picking (knee or elbow, it didn't matter).

By the 1970s I had matured a little. I didn't play conkers or marbles quite as often and if I created a slide in the snow then I did it surreptitiously, when I didn't think anyone was looking. But I retained my affection for nature; for the countryside, for animals, for birds and for everything alive whether it was running, flying, crawling or swimming.

And so living in Bilbury was a constant delight.

The countryside in North Devon was (and still is) wild, untamed, and as unspoilt as any area in England. In the 1970s, one or two farmers still used horses to pull their ploughs. The air was clean, fresh and healthy (it still is) and although a local hunt occasionally strayed into Bilbury in a usually unsuccessful search for a fox, the local wildlife had a pretty good time of it.

I strolled back along the lane, opened a small, wooden gate in the hedge and walked up a neat path to the front door of Buttercup Cottage. To my surprise, there was a holly wreath hanging from the door knocker. I wondered if the occupants knew the wreath was still there or if they had grown so accustomed to its presence that they didn't actually see it any more – in the way that someone might spend half an hour looking for their spectacles without realising that they were wearing them. I once spent twenty minutes looking for my car keys, and even enlisted Patsy's help, until she pointed out, with surprising patience, that I was holding them in my hand.

'Oh thank you for coming, doctor,' said a tiny woman who looked to be in her 60s. She had white hair, neatly done in a bun at the back, and wore silver framed reading glasses which were perched on the end of her nose. She was wearing a red and white dress with a floral pattern and over it she wore one of those old-fashioned pinafores which have a loop which goes over the head and

177

ties which can be knotted at the back of the waist. Her hands were covered with flour and she had a streak of flour on her left cheek. The pinafore had a picture of Father Christmas on the front. He was a very jolly, red-faced Father Christmas with a lot of white hair and a huge, white beard. I didn't really know why but she rather reminded me of a sparrow.

'Please excuse me, I didn't expect you to be here so quickly,' she said. 'I've been doing a little baking.' And then I realised why I had thought of a sparrow. She reminded me of Edith Piaf, the diminutive and legendary French singer.

I introduced myself, though this was clearly not really necessary since she obviously knew who I was. 'Mrs Thorley?'

'That's right. But it's my husband you've come to see.'

She opened the door wide and stepped back a couple of paces so that I could enter the cottage. It was one of those cottages which has low ceilings and very low doorways. I nearly always managed to bang my head at least once every time I entered one of those cottages.

As I entered the room, I could see that the Thorleys did not appear to have taken down any of their Christmas decorations. The holly wreath on the door was not an aberration. There were paper chains hanging from the ceiling (and making the ceiling appear even lower) and there were Christmas decorations on the mantelpiece. There was a beautifully decorated artificial tree in a corner of the room and a bunch of artificial mistletoe hung from the light fitting in the middle of the room. I was pleased to see a small crib, containing beautifully carved and painted, wooden figures, standing on a side table. The Thorleys had clearly not forgotten the purpose of the celebration which they had extended and appeared to be enjoying.

All this was made especially surprising since, at the time of my visit, it was a lovely, warm day in late May. The birds had done their nesting and were busy chasing about collecting food for their ever-hungry young ones.

It was surprising, and startling I suppose, because we tend to live by our traditions and habits because those give our lives a framework upon which to hang new experiences. When the traditions and habits are turned inside out, there is, for a moment or two, a tendency to feel rather lost.

Nevertheless, despite the incongruity, I couldn't help feeling a warm glow inside. Patsy and I always feel sad when twelfth night comes and it is time to put away the bits and pieces which help us to celebrate the festival period. We both love everything about Christmas.

'Would you like a mince pie and a glass of sherry?' Mrs Thorley asked. She pulled a tea towel out of the huge pocket on the front of her pinafore and wiped the flour off her hands. The tea towel was decorated with holly and little golden bells and other signs of Christmas.

'That's very kind of you. But maybe I should see your husband first?'

'Of course, doctor. He's in bed so I'll lead the way. Mind your step because the staircase is a little steep.'

Mrs Thorley opened what looked like a cupboard door and revealed one of those incredibly narrow and steep staircases with which small, old cottages often seem to be equipped. The stairs went almost straight up – more like a ladder than a normal staircase and the doorway into it was no more than five feet high and two feet wide. At the top of those tiny staircases, there are invariably just two rooms: one to the left and one to the right. Going up I found I always had to go sideways because the treads were no wider than the rungs of a ladder. Coming down, I always found very tricky – especially if I was holding something such as a black, medical bag. I found that the only safe way to descend was to treat the stairs just as I would have treated a ladder, and to come down backwards.

Thankfully, in the Thorley's cottage, someone had fixed rope bannisters on both sides of the staircase. The ropes were fixed to the wall at intervals of a yard and a half or so. I find rope bannisters rather fun and much more useful than old-fashioned wooden ones when climbing a steep and narrow staircase. The other advantage of rope bannisters is that in a narrow passageway they take up less room than traditional wooden bannisters.

Back in the days of Queen Elizabeth I, access to the upper floors in small cottages was via an ordinary ladder. When they were ready for bed, the occupants of the cottage would climb up their ladder and wriggle through a tiny hole in the ceiling. They would sleep in what would today be regarded as the attic or loft. People were smaller in those days, and more capable of scrambling up into small spaces. In the daytime, when it wasn't in use and would get in the way, the ladder was put out in the yard.

Some of the furniture used in those days was built in the bedroom and some, such as large wardrobes and four poster beds, came apart and had to be put together like large, three dimensional jigsaw puzzles. I have seen four poster beds that came apart and ended up as three or four dozen pieces of wood.

The big problem came when a patient died in their bedroom. I have known it to be necessary to remove a bedroom window and to take the deceased out that way. Windows which were big enough to take a coffin were known as 'coffin windows'.

I followed Mrs Thorley upstairs, banging my head on the top of the door frame as I did so. Someone, presumably Mrs Thorley, had tacked a piece of carpet to the door frame so the bang did me no harm and made no noise whatsoever. I couldn't help noticing that Mrs Thorley, who was scampering up the staircase like a mountain goat, was wearing slippers with a seasonal motif and ankle length socks which had little reindeers prancing about on them.

'Mind your head, doctor!' Mrs Thorley said, over her shoulder. She wasn't even bothering to hold onto the rope and did not seem to notice that the staircase was damned near vertical.

I promised, belatedly, that I would.

Mr Thorley was lying in bed reading.

I couldn't see all of him, of course, but he looked to be about the same age and same general size as his wife. It occurred to me that if you live in a small cottage, with low ceilings and a very narrow staircase, it helps if you're not too tall and not too wide.

The bedroom hadn't escaped the Christmas decorations.

Numerous, colourful streamers were stretched across the room, tied to picture frames and to tacks which had been hammered into walls and window frames. And although the bedroom was very small, there was another artificial Christmas tree in there. It was smaller than the tree downstairs but beautifully decorated with dozens of exquisite Victorian ornaments.

'We like Christmas,' said Mrs Thorley.

'I guessed!'

'It seems such a pity to take all the decorations down on twelfth night,' said Mr Thorley.

'We always hated putting them into their boxes and then packing them away into a cupboard,' said Mrs Thorley.

'So one year we just decided to leave them up,' continued Mr Thorley.

'I know it's supposed to be bad luck to leave them up after twelfth night,' said Mrs Thorley, 'but we've found a way to get round that.'

'We don't think of ourselves as leaving them up,' explained Mr Thorley. 'We think of ourselves as putting them up early for next Christmas.'

'We always take the fairies off the top of our trees on twelfth night,' said Mrs Thorley. 'And then we put them back on the next day.'

'We both like mince pies,' said Mr Thorley. 'And Christmas pudding.'

'And Christmas cake,' added Mrs Thorley. 'And sausage rolls.'

'Oh yes, I do like a sausage roll,' agreed Mr Thorley.

'A splendid idea!' I said. It seemed extraordinary that they weren't both hugely overweight.

I already liked the Thorleys. I liked them very much. Actually, it was pretty well impossible not to like them. They rather reminded me of a pair of children playing at life.

Mr Thorley made a fuss of wiping his cheek with his hand.

'What can I do for you?' I asked him.

'He's been very wobbly,' said Mrs Thorley.

Mr Thorley repeated the gesture. I guessed that he was quietly trying to tell his wife that she had flour on her cheek.

'For how long?'

'A month,' said Mrs Thorley. 'It seems to be getting worse.'

'Your cheek!' whispered Mr Thorley to his wife. He repeated the cheek-wiping gesture again.

Mrs Thorley realised what he was trying to tell her but she wiped the wrong cheek with the tea towel.

'Other one,' whispered Mr Thorley.

This time Mrs Thorley managed to wipe the flour off her cheek. 'Oh I'm so sorry, doctor,' she said. 'I'm really embarrassed now. What must you think of me?'

'Please don't give it a thought!' I said. 'When my wife bakes she usually ends up with flour on her face and in her hair. Actually, there is usually flour on the dog too. And I've been known to end up with flour on my face even if I've been out doing visits when she was baking.'

'Really?'

I smiled at her and nodded. 'Sometimes, people who are just walking past our house end up with flour on their noses.'

She laughed and relaxed a little.

'Apart from the wobbliness, do you have any health problems I should know about?' I asked Mr Thorley. 'Since you aren't actually a patient of mine I don't have any medical records for you.'

'He has high blood pressure,' said Mrs Thorley, who seemed to answer a lot for her husband. He didn't seem to mind that she did this.

'But who is treating that?' I asked, suddenly alarmed that I had seen Mr Thorley and forgotten him.

'We're still registered with our doctor in Exeter,' explained Mrs Thorley. 'That's where we used to live. Exeter.'

I was surprised by this. Exeter is the county town of Devon. It is over 60 miles away from Bilbury and it would take at least an hour and a half to drive from one to the other. That's quite a trek for a doctor to make in order to visit a patient.

'Does your doctor in Exeter still look after you both?' I asked.

'Well, we've been on his medical list since we left Exeter,' said Mrs Thorley. 'But when Mr Thorley was taken a bit poorly I telephoned his surgery and the receptionist told me that the doctor wouldn't visit us here because we are too far away. He told me that I had to telephone you.'

I wasn't surprised. 'Do you take any tablets?' I asked Mr Thorley.

'Oh yes. I have the pills for my blood pressure. But I've always had those.'

'You get them from your doctor in Exeter?'

'I do. Every three months I send in a request together with a stamped addressed envelope and the doctor sends me a prescription for another supply of my pills.'

'I take the prescription into Boots the chemist in Barnstaple,' said Mrs Thorley.

'When did you have your blood pressure taken last?' I asked Mr Thorley.

'Just before we moved from Exeter.'

'Not since then?'

'Oh no. Our doctor told us that I would need to keep taking the tablets for the rest of my life so there didn't seem any need to have it taken again.'

'Ah,' I said.

This was rather startling news.

Patients who have high blood pressure need to have readings taken regularly since it is not at all impossible for blood pressure to change quite dramatically over a few months – let alone three years. And a change in circumstances can have a tremendous effect on the blood pressure. It wasn't difficult to guess that the Thorleys lived a rather different life in Bilbury to the life they'd lived in Exeter.

I opened my black bag and took out my sphygmomanometer and my stethoscope. 'Roll up your pyjama sleeve, please, Mr Thorley.'

Mr Thorley rolled up his sleeve. It was very loose and rolled up out of the way quite easily.

'You've been dizzy?' I asked, as I wrapped the cuff around his upper arm.

'Oh yes, doctor. Very dizzy.'

'And when he gets out of bed he falls down,' said Mrs Thorley. 'With our stairs it's very dangerous. I've made him stay in bed.'

I took Mr Thorley's blood pressure.

I then took it again.

And I then took it for a third time.

Now, usually, when a doctor or a nurse takes a patient's blood pressure the reading is a little higher than it is normally. The very presence of the doctor or nurse, and the fact that they are taking the blood pressure, can push it up quite noticeably.

But Mr Thorley's blood pressure as he lay in bed was 90 over 65. For a man of his age that was very low and meant that his systolic pressure was 30 points lower than the normal for a young, healthy man. And since his blood pressure would fall when he stood up I could see why he was falling down every time he got out of bed.

'Could I see the pills you are taking?' I asked.

Mrs Thorley picked a bottle of pills off the nearest of the two bedside tables and handed the bottle to me.

They were a popularly prescribed and powerful drug for high blood pressure.

'I think you may need to reduce your drug dosage,' I told him, tactfully. 'It seems that the pills you are taking have reduced your blood pressure rather too far.'

'Oh I don't think my doctor would like that,' said Mr Thorley, rather nervously. 'He did say that I would need to take the pills for the rest of my life.'

'Maybe Mr Thorley needs to take a higher dose?' suggested Mrs Thorley, clearly trying to be helpful.

'Am I right in thinking that you are retired, now?' I asked her husband.

'Oh yes,' said Mr Thorley. 'Very definitely.'

'We came here when Mr Thorley retired,' added Mrs Thorley. 'We wanted to get away.'

'Too many people knew me down there,' said Mr Thorley. His wife reached out and patted his hand.

'May I ask what you did for a living?' I asked Mr Thorley.

He looked at his wife and she looked back at him. They were both obviously reluctant to tell me.

'Would you say it was a stressful job?' I asked.

They looked at each other.

'Oh yes, very much,' said Mrs Thorley.

'Quite definitely,' said Mr Thorley.

I waited, assuming that one or the other would tell me what the job had been. But this clearly wasn't on the agenda. 'But now that you're living here that stress has gone?'

'Oh yes,' said Mrs Thorley. 'We like it here very much. We don't go out much, of course, but we like it here.'

'Because of my job,' said Mr Thorley, as though in explanation.

'You don't go out much because of what you did for a living when you lived in Exeter?'

'That's right.'

I began to wonder what on earth Mr Thorley had done for a living when they were living in Exeter. What on earth had attracted such opprobrium? What sort of employment could have possibly affected them so much that they were, even now, frightened to show themselves? I couldn't think of anything that could be as bad as they seemed to think it was. There hadn't been a hangman in England for decades.

'Well, whatever it was, it's all over now,' I said to Mr Thorley. If they didn't want to tell me what he did for a living then that was fine with me. 'And it's a reasonable guess that your job caused, or at least contributed to, your high blood pressure.'

'Oh yes, that's what our doctor in Exeter told us,' said Mrs Thorley. 'But he...'

'...said that Mr Thorley would need to take the blood pressure tablets for the rest of his life,' I said, finishing the sentence for her.

'That's right.'

'Well, I'm sure that your doctor in Exeter would agree with me that since Mr Thorley is now retired, and is free of the stress associated with his former job, then he won't need to take as many pills for his blood pressure. In fact, he may be able to stop the pills completely!'

'Oh, the doctor wouldn't like that!' said Mrs Thorley firmly.

I couldn't help feeling that the conversation wasn't getting me anywhere.

'May I ask you why you asked me to call today?'

'Because Mr Thorley is very dizzy,' explained Mrs Thorley, rather patiently. 'When he gets out of bed he falls over.'

'And remind me, please, why your doctor in Exeter didn't come to visit you.'

'He says we live too far away.'

'Didn't he suggest that you should register with another doctor?'

'No!' said Mrs Thorley. 'He said he would keep providing us with pills but that if we needed a visit we should call a local doctor.'

'And you did call me and I have suggested that Mr Thorley needs to cut down his pills.'

'Yes, but you're not our proper doctor,' said Mrs Thorley, with the definitiveness of a woman who has produced the ace of trumps.

I took a deep breath and waited a moment before continuing. 'I think you are going to have to telephone your doctor,' I said at last. 'You need to speak to him and ask him if he wants to continue looking after you both in your new home. If he is going to continue to dictate your treatment then he really needs to be in charge of doing things like taking blood pressures and so on.'

'All right, doctor,' said Mrs Thorley. She scuttled off to the top of the stairs and a moment later I heard her going down to the living room where, I assumed, the telephone was situated.

'I was a traffic warden,' said Mr Thorley, suddenly.

I looked at him.

'That was my job.'

'Ah,' I said, beginning to understand.

'I wasn't always a traffic warden,' he said. 'When I was young I worked as a human cannon ball in a circus in Blackpool. Just for a season.' He managed a small smile. 'I was fired every day and twice on Saturdays.'

'Not a job you could rely on, then?'

'No. In the end, I was fired permanently. The manager said I wasn't any good at it. Apparently I always used to look relieved after I'd been shot out of the cannon and had landed safely. He said they wanted someone who smiled a bit more and waved to the crowd. I was always too relieved to do much waving and smiling.'

'Seems a bit much,' I said. 'Expecting you to be fired from a cannon and to smile about it afterwards.'

'That's what I thought,' said Mr Thorley with a sigh. 'They hired a girl to replace me. She was very curvy, well-built in the bosom department, and she managed to arrange it so that her top always fell off when she landed. That went down very well with the audience. She always managed to make it look as though it were all accidental and had embarrassed her. I was demoted to working on the candy floss stall.'

'And did the new human cannon ball smile as well as lose her top?'

'Oh yes, very much so.'

'So then you became a traffic warden?'

'Eventually, yes. I had a few other jobs in between. I worked on a trawler but discovered I got seasick. I parked cars for a five star hotel in the West End of London and I worked as a messenger for a firm of solicitors. I was a chauffeur too, for a while. But after I met Mrs Thorley I needed to settle down. And being a traffic warden seemed a good, steady, reliable job.'

'Just the ticket, eh?'

He looked at me, puzzled.

'But it didn't turn out very satisfactorily?' I said, moving on quickly.

'No, the people in our street knew I was a traffic warden and they gave us both a hard time about it.'

'How did they find out?'

'I went to work every morning in my uniform.'

'Ah. I suppose that would give it away. And your neighbours didn't like traffic wardens?'

'No. My boss sent me to work in our street on a couple of occasions.'

'I see.'

And I did. I hadn't always been appreciative of the work done by traffic wardens. It must have been very difficult for Mr and Mrs Thorley. It seemed particularly unfair to send the fellow to give out parking tickets in the street where he lived.

'The neighbours were especially unpleasant after I had to give several of them parking tickets.'

'I can see why that wouldn't make you the most popular man in the street.'

'It didn't.'

'And did you like anything about the work?'

'No. I hated it. But I couldn't find any other employment.'

'But you're not a traffic warden now,' I said.

'No. I'm retired. I came back from work one day, took off my cap and told Mrs Thorley that I couldn't do it anymore. A woman had screamed at me and said some awful things. I told Mrs Thorley that I'd get another job. I said I'd rather clean lavatories than be a traffic warden.' He swallowed and there were tears in his eyes. 'But Mrs Thorley said I had worked hard all my life and that I should retire and that we would move away and buy a cottage in the country. I said we didn't have enough money put aside to retire but she said she'd been saving hard out of the housekeeping and putting aside as much as she could from her wages from cleaning in the supermarket and that there was enough for us to retire if we cut our cloth according to our means. She said we would get a good price for our little house because Exeter had become quite an expensive place to live, and the area where we lived was quite fashionable, and she was right and we sold the car too and we looked around and found this little cottage here in Bilbury. And we've never had expensive habits so we've been able to manage.'

'Do you feel less stressed now that you're no longer a traffic warden?'

'Oh yes, I do. Oh yes, I most certainly do.'

'And the people in Bilbury don't know that you were a traffic warden and since you are no longer a traffic warden they wouldn't give a fig if they did,' I pointed out.

Mr Thorley accepted these words with some surprise. And then slowly, very slowly, a smile crept across his face. 'Do you think so?'

'I'm sure so,' I said.

'Oh,' said Mr Thorley. 'Well, that's quite a relief. Can I tell Mrs Thorley that? I think she'll be relieved too.'

'Of course you can!'

I really did like the Thorleys. They were what used to be called a 'sweet couple'. I find that if you talk to older people they always, but always, have fascinating stories to share. The young frequently dismiss the elderly as boring but they would learn a good deal if they had the patience to listen occasionally.

Just then Mrs Thorley reappeared. She looked rather cross.

'Well,' she said. And then she repeated it with an exclamation mark after it. 'Well!' Finally, she said it again with two exclamation marks. 'Well!!'

'What did your doctor in Exeter have to say?' I asked her.

'He was very rude!' said Mrs Thorley, who seemed quite surprised at this. 'He said he wasn't going to visit us up here in North Devon and that he'd only kept us on his list as a favour but that if I was going to be difficult then we could find another doctor and good riddance to us!'

I didn't point out their doctor in Exeter might, just might, have kept them on his list because in the National Health Service a doctor is paid according to the number of patients who are registered with him. Their Exeter doctor was earning money for doing nothing more than sign repeat prescriptions occasionally.

'So what do you want to do?' I asked them both.

'Well, we have to find another doctor,' said Mrs Thorley. 'We need a doctor so that we can obtain Mr Thorley's prescriptions.'

'Mr Thorley might not need his prescriptions,' I pointed out.

Mrs Thorley looked at me rather suspiciously.

I smiled at her. 'You must choose a new doctor,' I told her. 'There are doctors in Barnstaple and Combe Martin who would probably take you onto their lists.'

'But you're the only doctor in Bilbury,' said Mrs Thorley.

'That's not a very good reason to choose a doctor,' I told her.

'No, I suppose it isn't,' she agreed.

'Can we try you on approval?' asked Mr Thorley, rather nervously.

'You mean, can you sign up with me and then change to another doctor in a week or two if you're unhappy with me?'

'That's sort of what I meant,' said Mr Thorley.

'Of course you can,' I said.

'You wouldn't mind?'

'Not at all! I don't want to look after patients who aren't happy with having me as their doctor.'

'Well, that's settled then,' said Mrs Thorley. She looked at her husband. He nodded. 'We'll take you on approval.'

I thanked them both and said that since I was now their doctor, albeit 'on approval', I wanted Mr Thorley to cut his pills down by a quarter.

'That's almost certainly not going to be a sharp enough cut to make the dizziness go away,' I told him. 'But if we're going to make changes than we need to do them slowly. I'll pop in to check Mr Thorley's blood pressure in a couple of days and we'll see how things are then.'

They seemed unhappy about this but said they'd try it.

'Meanwhile,' I told Mr Thorley. 'You must be very cautious when getting out of bed. And when you walk about you must hold onto things. And when you go down the stairs you'd probably better go down on your bottom; just bumping your bottom from one step to the next.'

'Oh dear,' said Mrs Thorley. She looked at her husband. 'Are you happy about all this, Mr Thorley?' she asked him.

He said he was.

Mrs Thorley then nodded her approval.

'Would you like that mince pie now, doctor?' she asked. 'And a glass of sherry, perhaps?'

'I'd be delighted to try one of your mince pies,' I told her. 'And I'd be very pleased to celebrate our new partnership, albeit on approval, with a very small glass of sherry.'

Mrs Thorley hurried off again to the stairs.

'We like Christmas very much,' said Mr Thorley rather unnecessarily.

'So I gathered.'

From the bedroom window I could see a camellia bush. It was laden with beautiful pink camellias. And on a bird table down below, a robin was feeding what looked like sunflower hearts to a hungry youngster. The sun was shining and spring was already in full swing. I could hear a blackbird singing its heart out somewhere in a rhododendron bush.

Downstairs Mrs Thorley switched on a record player and I could hear the wonderful, if slightly anachronistic, sound of Harry Belafonte singing *Mary's Boy Child*.

'Mrs Thorley is going to be very pleased about our not having to hide away,' whispered Mr Thorley.

And I am delighted to report that everything turned out well.

Five weeks later, to my delight, I was finally able to wean Mr Thorley off the last of his blood pressure pills.

And two days after that a very healthy Carlton and Hermione Thorley came to see me at Bilbury Grange to tell me that they had decided that I was no longer on approval. They brought me a dozen mince pies and two large slices of Christmas cake.

The mince pies and the Christmas cake were very tasty and most enjoyable, although Patsy and I agreed that it did seem a little strange to be eating mince pies and Christmas cake in the middle of the summer.

Author's Note 1:
Thank you for your company. I hope you have enjoyed this book about Bilbury. If you did so then I would be very grateful if you would spare a moment to write a short review. It really helps a lot.
Thank you
Vernon Coleman

Author's Note 2:
Mr Fish's poems, quoted in the text of this book, are reproduced with permission. A fee has been paid to Mr Fish's estate and the proceeds distributed, according to his will, to Charlene Jackson (nee Walkinshaw) of Barnstaple. Charlene is the daughter of Charlotte, the former girlfriend mentioned in the memory about Mr Fish. Although Mr Fish met her only once, and then just for a few moments, he left his entire estate to her.

The Appendices

Appendix No 1: Tea-Time Treats

1. Bakewell Pudding is an English dessert which consists of a flaky pastry base upon which has been placed a layer of jam and a filling made out of egg and almond paste. There are probably as many local variations on this theme as there are local cake shops but it is generally agreed that the Pudding was first made by accident in the 1820s by a cook who was or was not working at a hostelry which might or might not have been called the White Horse Inn. (As with most such bits and pieces of social history, the only certainty is that there is no certainty.) The cook was allegedly told to make a jam tart but, according to legend, instead of stirring the eggs and almond paste mixture into the pastry (as she might have been expected to do) she put the jam onto the pastry base and placed the almond paste on top of the jam. She was probably pleasantly tiddly at the time. When the whole thing came out of the oven, the cook found herself an unexpected heroine and her serendipitous creation became a popular dish at the inn. Incidentally, no other town in England has both a tart and a pudding named after it and in that respect Bakewell is unique.
2. Bakewell Tart is a thoroughly English confection which consists of a short-crust pastry base or case filled with a layer of jam and a sponge which is made with ground almonds (known to aficionados as frangipane). A Cherry Bakewell is a commercial variation of the traditional tart and has the frangipane covered with a layer of white, almond-flavoured fondant blessed with half a glace cherry.
3. Banbury Cake: First made by Edward Welchman in the 17th century, Banbury cakes are made with currants, mixed peel, brown sugar, rum and nutmeg.
4. Bath Bun: First produced in 1763 by Dr Oliver, a doctor who treated patients at the Bath Spa. The bun, created to be eaten in the

192

baths, was so popular that patients who ate too many put on weight. And so the Bath Oliver biscuit was invented as a substitute.

5. Chelsea Bun: Chelsea buns were first sold at the Chelsea Bun House in central London. Both Jonathan Swift and Charles Dickens bought buns there. (The shop is mentioned in Dickens's books *Barnaby Rudge* and *Bleak House*.) A Chelsea Bun is made of a roll of raisin-spotted dough which contains cinnamon. The roll of dough is made into a square bun but can be unrolled to be eaten.

6. Chorley Cake: First made in Chorley in Lancashire a Chorley Cake is similar to an Eccles cake but is made with currants between two layers of unsweetened short-crust pastry and commonly served with butter on top.

7. Crumpet: The original crumpets were small, oval cakes made with unsweetened batter which contained water and flour. These were also known as picklets or pikelets. From Victorian times onwards, crumpets or pikelets contained yeast and bicarbonate of soda and became soft and spongy.

8. Eccles Cake: Originated in Eccles, near Manchester and was first made in 1796. The ingredients are squashed, juicy raisins in a flaky pastry.

9. Gloucester Tart: Made in Gloucester on the edge of the Cotswolds. It is identical to a Bakewell Tart except that ground rice is added to the ingredients.

10. Muffin: There are two types of muffin. The original muffin was a flatbread bun dating back to before the 18th century. These are known in the US as English muffins. The cupcake muffin originated in North America in the 19th century.

11. Teacake: In the UK, a teacake is a yeast based sweet bun containing dried fruit and usually toasted and served with butter. In the US, a teacake can be a biscuit or a small cake. There are many different types of English teacake – varying from the manchet (or Lady Arundel's Manchet) which is popular in Sussex and made with nutmeg, cinnamon and rose water to the huffkin (which is made in Kent and flavoured with hops).

12. Welsh cakes: Traditional snacks from Wales. The ingredients are flour, sultanas and raisins. Welsh cakes look like scones but are smaller, flatter and softer.

Appendix 2: Ten Diseases Related to Occupations

In the memory entitled *Iolanthe and Bertie in River Cottage* I describe Farmers' Lung, a dangerous and sometimes deadly condition known to be an occupational hazard of those working on farms. Farmers' Lung still occurs and is still as deadly as ever. There are, of course, many other disorders which are, or were, associated with particular trades and professions. Here are ten of the best known:

1. 'Hatter's Shakes' was not something invented by Lewis Carroll for the Mad Hatter. It was a very real condition which affected those working in the hat trade. The symptoms were caused by the mercury which was used in curing the felt from which hats were made.

2. 'Painters colic' was a condition affecting house painters. It was caused by the lead which was a common ingredient of many paints.

3. 'Miner's nystagmus' was a condition affecting those who spent long hours working underground.

4. 'Glassblower's cataract' was a form of cataract caused by exposure to the glare from molten glass. Modern glassblowers avoid the problem by wearing special goggles.

5. 'Grocer's itch' is a type of dermatitis caused by mites in the grain handled by those in the grocery trade.

6. 'Asbestosis' was a lung condition commonly found among those working with asbestos. Regulations now control the use of asbestos.

7. 'Office worker's sinus' – is a name given to sinus troubles caused by working in air conditioned offices where the air is over-dried by the air conditioning.

8. 'Typists' Mastitis' was a condition which affected female typists. The condition, an inflammation of the breast, was caused by the constant operation of the carriage lever on a manual typewriter. Since manual typewriters are now used only rarely, the condition is also rare.

9. 'Lorry Drivers' Gastritis' is a stomach condition caused by the enthusiasm of lorry drivers for 'greasy spoon' cafés. Lorry drivers also tend to suffer a good deal from bad backs.

10. 'Dentist's Veins' – dentists, shop assistants and others who spent much of their day standing up used to be exceptionally likely to develop varicose veins. Today, many dentists sit down while they are working – as do many shop assistants.

Appendix 3: The Battle of Naseby

In my chapter about Logan Berry, I mentioned that vanity has often had a great impact on history. Few events in history illustrate the dangers of vanity as much as the Battle of Naseby.

The Battle of Naseby took place on the 14th June 1645 near to the village of Naseby in Northamptonshire. It was the decisive battle in the English Civil War. On one side was the Royalist army of King Charles I and on the other was the Parliamentarian New Model Army which was commanded by Oliver Cromwell and Sir Thomas Fairfax.

The King himself had insisted on being present on the battlefield and, vain to the point of lunacy, he had turned up clad in a gilt plated suit of armour. Naturally, he was the only person on the battlefield wearing golden armour and he was a clear target for the Parliamentarians who were attacking and winning the battle. One of the King's attendants, realising the vulnerability of his monarch, forced Charles to wheel his horse to one side to escape the fighting. Unfortunately, this fairly innocent movement was misinterpreted as a signal to the whole front line of the Royalist forces. When they saw the King's golden armour on the move, everyone else followed.

The result, as the Royalist army struggled to wheel in order to follow the King, was a very fatal chaos and confusion. Cromwell led his army forward in a final, glorious charge and the King's forces were in such disarray that they had no choice but to retreat. The Royal losses were massive for a battle at that time. Around 1,000 men were killed and five times as many were captured. More importantly, perhaps, the King's private papers were captured. These papers revealed the King's attempt to bring foreign mercenaries into the war and helped to strengthen support for the Parliamentarians. The King never again managed to put a sizeable force into the field and within a year, Cromwell and Fairfax had won the Civil War.

It is no exaggeration to say that one man's vanity, and that silly golden armour, changed English history.

Appendix 4: Slobberdochers, Slammerkins and Cachinnators

While my friend William was staying at Bilbury Grange he and I created another one of our lists of unusual words.

The list that follows is as comprehensive a list as we could compile of colourful words, many of them rather Rabelaisian, which describe various types of individual.

It should be noted that since this list was created in the 1970s, it does not include any terms which came into use after that decade.

Bawdy – an obscene or lewd individual
Blockhead – a stupid or foolish person
Braggard – a boaster
Cachinnator – someone who laughs loudly
Changeling – a fairy child left in the place of a real child
Cockalorum – little man with a high opinion of himself
Cotquean – a man doing a woman's work
Curmudgeon – a bad tempered old man
Dandiprat – anything (or anyone) small
Daphlean – a shy and beautiful person (usually female)
Deipnosophist – someone skilled in making dinner table conversation
Dell – a girl
Demi-lass – a polite word for a trollop, slut or slag
Demirep – someone with no reputation at all
Doxies – morts who are neither married nor virgins
Druggel – a mangy rascal
Flaneur – someone who saunters and observes
Franion – a licentious person
Fraters – fraudulent collectors for charity
Freshwater mariners – bogus old sailors
Galliard – a man of fashion
Gangrel – a loafing lout
Goosecap – a silly person (especially a flighty, young girl)
Gripple – a mean or stingy person

Grouthead – a stupid fellow, a blockhead
Hobbledehoy – a clumsy youth
Hooker – a woman who sells her body
Horbgorbler – someone who potters about in an ineffective way
Hornswoggler – a cheat
Hoydon – a romping girl
Hypergelast – someone who laughs excessively
Jarkman – a sham clergyman, someone who specialises in false marriages
Jejune – naïve, simplistic
Jezebel – an immoral, dishonest woman
Jolthead – a stupid or foolish person
Kinching morts – female juvenile delinquents
Knave – a deceitful or tricky fellow
Larrikin – a maverick; a boisterous, badly behaved person
Lobcock – a stupid, blundering person
Lob-dotterel – a gullible fool
Lout – an uncouth or aggressive man
Lungis – a tall and clumsy man
Lusk – a sloth
Maltworm – a drinker
Mangie – a rascal
Marmalade madam – a strumpet
Marmulet – a strumpet
Meacock – an effeminate man; a man without spirit
Miffy – a fit of peevish ill humour
Mignon – dainty
Milksop – an indecisive individual, lacking courage
Mizzling – sauntering, moving slowly
Moonling – a dreamy fool
Moppet – a peach or kitten of a girl
Mort – a girl
Mountebank – a charlatan, a deceiver
Muffishness – soft and effeminate
Mugwump – someone who backs down, withdraws
Mumchance – silent or tongue tied
Myrmidon – an unscrupulous follower
Necromancer – a wizard or magician
Ninnyhammer – a fool or simpleton

Oaf – a rough or clumsy man (usually also unintelligent)
Oddling – a lonely, strange person
Ombompom – well bosomed
Palliard – a beggar, usually rather scruffy
Panegyrist – someone who speaks or writes in praise of another
Pantywaist – an effeminate or feeble person
Patrico – a sham clergyman
Pimp – a man who manages prostitutes and lives off their earnings
Poltroon – a coward
Popinjay – a vain or conceited person who dresses extravagantly
Prancer – a horse thief
Pretty – a gallant; an alert, prompt fellow always ready for action
Prigger – a horse thief
Rogue – a dishonest or unprincipled man
Roly poly – a short, plump person of either sex
Ruffler – someone pretending to be an old soldier, etc.
Scobberlotcher – an idler
Shill – a confidence trickster's accomplice
Slag – a worthless person (usually female)
Slaister – someone who slaps on lots of make-up
Slammerkin – a slattern
Slubberdegullion – a dirty, worthless, careless fellow
Slut – a woman who has many casual sexual partners
Spindle-shanks – a person with long thin legs
Tart – a woman who is obviously sexually available
Titivil – a knave
Tittup – someone with a mincing, prancing gait
Toothsome –voluptuous and alluring
Tretis – well-proportioned and graceful
Trollop – a sluttish woman
Uncumber – a bearded woman with holy attributes (St Uncumber
was a bearded woman and the benefactress of wives; according to
Sir Thomas More she would, if given a peck of oats, provide a horse
upon which an evil husband could ride to the devil)
Uprightmen – top rogues
Vagabond – a wanderer
Vamp – a seductress or femme fatale
Venecund – shy and bashful
Venust – beautiful and elegant

Virago – a bad tempered, violent, domineering woman
Walking mort – a female vagabond
Wanton – ungoverned, rebellious
Whore – a woman who sells her body
Zaftig – having a pleasantly plump figure

Appendix 5: The English Spirit

Many of my memories contain examples of 'the English Spirit' – a refusal to be bowed by disappointment and adversity.

The determination to remain cool in trying or dangerous circumstances, is of course, a very traditional English response to the exigencies of life. Oddly enough, a French word (sangfroid – which literally means 'cold blood') is often used to describe it. Since sangfroid is not usually regarded as a French virtue this is rather inexplicable.

There are many examples of The English Spirit (or the stiff upper lip) in history. Here are a few:

Samuel Pepys, the diarist, wrote about seeing Major General Harrison remaining cheerful and jolly when he was about to be hung, drawn and quartered at Charing Cross. Only a true Englishman could make jokes as he waited to have his intestines dragged out of his body and burnt before his very eyes.

(The first part of the triple punishment known as being 'hung, drawn and quartered' involved the hanging of the prisoner until he was almost dead. The poor devil would then be taken off the scaffold, still alive, and put on a table. His intestines would be surgically removed and burnt on a bonfire close to him so that he could watch them burning. Only then would he be chopped into five pieces – the four quarters of the body and the head – so that the bits could be displayed in different parts of the town.)

And then there was the Earl of Uxbridge who, on the battlefield of Waterloo, turned to the Duke of Wellington and said: 'Begad, Sir, I've lost me leg!' To which the Iron Duke replied: 'By God, Sir, so you have.'

Thirdly, there was Captain Lawrence Edward Grace Oates.

Oates was a member of the Terra Nova expedition led by Robert Falcon Scott and intended to reach the South Pole. During the ill-fated expedition, Oates developed frostbite and gangrene. Realising that his ill health was compromising the chances of his three companions surviving, he walked out of their small tent into a blizzard and died on his 32nd birthday.

Scott, who also died on the expedition, wrote in his diary that as Oates left the tent, heading for certain death, he turned to his companions and said: 'I am just going outside and may be some time.'

As an example of the English Spirit, it is impossible to beat.

Appendix 6: Epitaphs: Genuine Gravestone inscriptions

If you wander around old English graveyards you will often find old headstones which bear long inscriptions. (Either it was a lot cheaper to find a mason to do the chiselling or else people were prepared to spend a good deal of their savings on paying for the work to be done.) Here are a few epitaphs taken from English churchyards and revealed in W.H.Hudson's book *Traveller in Little Things*, which contains an essay on epitaphs entitled *A Haunter of Churchyards*.

1

(Taken from a churchyard at Maddington in Wiltshire and dated 1843)
These few lines have been procured
To tell the pains which he endured
He was crushed to death by the fall
Of an old mould'ring, tottering wall.

2

(Taken from a churchyard at Mylor, Cornwall, undated)
His foot it slipped and he did fall
Help! Help! He cried, and that was all

3

(Taken from a churchyard in Lynn, dated 1712)
He hath gained his port and is at ease,
And hath escapt ye danger of ye seas
His glass is run, his life is gone

4

(Taken from a churchyard in Minturne Magna, Dorset, dated 1805)
Neighbours make no stay,
Return unto the lord,
Nor put it off from day to day,
For Death's a debt ye all must pay.

Ye knoweth not how soon,
It may be the next moment,
Night, morning or noon.
I set this as a caution
To my neighbours in rime,
God give grace that you
May all repent in time.
For what God has decreed
We surely must obey,
For when please God to send
His death's dart into us so keen
O then we must go hence
And be no more here seen

5

(Taken from a churchyard in Kew, dated 1728)
At Tyre they were born and bred
And in the same good lives they led,
Until they come to married state,
Which was to them most fortunate.
Near sixty years of mortal life
They were a happy man and wife
And being so by Nature tyed
When one fell sich the other dyed,
And both together laid in dust
To await the rising of the just.
They had six children born and bred,
And five before them being dead,
Their only then surviving son
Hath caused this stone for to be done.

6

(Taken from a churchyard in St Just, Cornwall, dated 1771)
Life's but a snare, a Labyrnth of Woe
Which wretched Man is doomed to struggle through.
Today he's great, tomorrow he's undone,
And thus with Hope and Fear he blunders on,
Till some disease, or else perhaps old Age
Calls us poor Mortals trembling from the Stage.

7
(Taken from a churchyard in Lelant, Cornwall and undated)
What now you are so once was me,
What now I am that you will be,
Therefore prepare to follow me

Appendix 7: John 'Babbacombe' Lee: The Man They Couldn't Hang

For a while, a pub in London had a placard on the wall inviting patrons 'to be served by the man they could not hang'.

The man serving ale in the pub was John Henry George Lee, otherwise known as John 'Babbacombe' Lee, and he was famous for surviving three attempts to hang him for murder.

Born in Devon in 1864, Lee was employed by Miss Emma Keyse as a footman at her home at Babbacombe Bay, near Torquay in Devon. Although the evidence was weak, Lee, a known thief, was convicted of robbing Miss Keyse, beating her to death and then setting fire to the house in order to wipe out all traces of his crime. Lee claimed that he was innocent but he was not believed and he was sentenced to be hung.

On February 23rd in 1885. Three attempts were made to hang Lee at the prison in Exeter. All three attempts failed because the scaffold trapdoor failed to open on each occasion. Between attempts, the hangman, James Berry tested the scaffold with a bag of sand which was the same weight as the man to be hung. And with the bag of sand the scaffold worked perfectly well.

In the end, the medical officer, Dr T Wilson Gaird, refused to have anything more to do with the proceedings which were then halted. The Home Secretary later commuted Lee's sentence to life imprisonment.

There was much confusion about why the execution failed.

Lee claimed that he was saved by divine intervention but later investigations showed that there was a more earthly explanation.

There was no proper scaffold at Exeter (or indeed at any other provincial prisons in England) and all the paraphernalia required was kept at Pentonville prison in London and moved to Exeter beforehand. A special flooring was created with a pit below which allowed a drop of eight feet and an experienced hangman.

When everything was ready, Lee was taken into the execution room together with the usual impressive array of officials, observers and notables: the Governor, the chaplain, the doctor, representatives of the press and so on. And, of course, the experienced hangman whose name was James Berry. (Incidentally, Berry used to make extra money by cutting up the ropes he used and selling the pieces to those who collected such grisly relics.)

The noose was put around Lee's neck and a white bag was put over his head.

But when the lever was pulled, the trapdoor did not open and Lee was left standing on the trap with the noose hanging loosely around his neck.

Everyone was ushered out and carpenters were called in. They shaved some wood from the side of the trap. Lee was brought back, together with all the officials, and the noose was put around his neck again. The hangman then pulled the lever.

Once again, nothing happened. Lee stood there, on the trap, immobile.

So once again, the noose was taken from around Lee's neck and everyone was ushered out of the room.

This time, the hangman tested the apparatus with the sandbag.

Everything worked perfectly.

And so Lee was brought back for a third time, together with all the officials. Once again, the noose was put around John Lee's neck and the hangman pulled the lever.

And for the third time the trapdoor failed to open.

It was at this point that the medical officer walked out and the condemned man was sent back to his cell while the Governor used the new-fangled telephone to communicate with the Home Office. The Home Secretary decreed that Lee should be reprieved but kept in prison. And so Lee was put into a uniform with broad arrows on it and eventually sent to Dartmoor.

The subsequent investigation showed that the trap worked perfectly well when there were no spectators gathered around but that when the Governor, the doctor, the chaplain, members of the press and various other dignitaries crowded onto the platform, the floor expanded and prevented the trapdoor from opening.

Naturally, Lee insisted that he was an innocent man. He repeatedly petitioned successive Home Secretaries, demanding that he be released and eventually, after 21 years, he was released. Physically and mentally he showed signs of his experience. After his release, Lee went to London where he worked in a pub – promoted as 'the man they couldn't hang'. For a while, Lee made a living out of his notoriety (giving talks and even appearing in a silent film) but eventually he married a nurse and made his way to the United States where, apparently tiring of the notoriety, he lived quietly. He died in 1945 at the age of 80 and is believed to be buried in Forest Home Cemetery in Milwaukee.

The only other man to have survived three hanging attempts was called Joseph Samuel. He was English but was transported to Australia in 1801 for robbery. A couple of years later Samuel was convicted of murdering a policeman (a crime he denied) and, like Lee, he was sentenced to be hung. In Australia, they used a slightly different method for hanging. Nooses were fastened around the prisoners' necks and tied to a gallows while the prisoners stood on a cart. The cart was then driven away and the prisoners were left hanging and slowly strangling. (The English method was designed to be quicker; to produce a sudden drop which broke the neck.)

On the first attempt, the rope (made of five cords of hemp and designed to hold 1,000 lbs without breaking) snapped and Samuel fell and sprained his ankle. On the second attempt, the noose slipped off Samuel's neck. The third attempt was equally unsuccessful since as the cart was driven away the rope snapped and Samuel again fell to the ground.

An angry and boisterous crowd called for Samuel to be let go. The governor, when called to the scene, decided that God had intervened and commuted Samuel's sentence to life imprisonment. The local doctor looked after Samuel's sprained ankle, which was all he had to show for three hanging attempts. Samuel survived only another three years.

The Author

Vernon Coleman is an author and doctor. His novels include: *Mrs Caldicot's Cabbage War*, *Mrs Caldicot's Knickerbocker Glory*, *Mrs Caldicot's Easter Parade*, *Mr Henry Mulligan'*, *The Truth Kills*, *Second Chance*, *Paris in my Springtime*, *It's Never Too Late*, *The Hotel Doctor*, *My Secret Years with Elvis* and many others. All of these books are available as ebooks on Amazon. All the books in 'The Young Country Doctor' series are available as ebooks on Amazon.

Before you go…

Thank you for your company. Sorry to go on about it, and apologies if you already have done so, but if you have enjoyed this volume in The Young Country Doctor series, I really would be very grateful if you would spare a moment to write a short review.

Thank you

Vernon Coleman

Made in the USA
Middletown, DE
20 May 2021